200

5:2 DIET RECIPES

D0544537

HAMLYN **ALL COLOUR COOKBOOK**

200

5:2 DIET RECIPES

An Hachette UK Company
www.hachette.co.uk

First published in Great Britain in 2014 by Hamlyn,
a division of Octopus Publishing Group Ltd,
Carmelite House, 50 Victoria Embankment,
London EC4Y 0DZ
www.octopusbooks.co.uk

This edition published in 2016

ISBN 978-0-600-63347-1

A CIP catalogue record for this book is available
from the British Library

Printed and bound in China

10 9 8 7 6 5 4 3 2 1

Standard level spoon measurement are used in all recipes.
1 tablespoon = one 15 ml spoon
1 teaspoon = one 5 ml spoon

Both imperial and metric measures have been given in
all recipes. Use one set of measurements only and not a
mixture of both.

Eggs should be medium unless otherwise stated. The
Department of Health advises that eggs should not be
consumed raw. This book contains dishes made with raw
or lightly cooked eggs. It is prudent for more vulnerable
people such as pregnant and nursing mothers, invalids,
the elderly, babies and young children to avoid uncooked
or lightly cooked dishes made with eggs. Once prepared
these dishes should be kept refrigerated and used promptly.

Ovens should be preheated to the specific temperature
– if using a fan-assisted oven, follow the manufacturer's
instructions for adjusting the time and the temperature.

This book includes dishes made with nuts and nut
derivatives. It is advisable for customers with known allergic
reactions to nuts and nut derivatives and those who may be
potentially vulnerable to these allergies, such as pregnant
and nursing mothers, invalids, the elderly, babies and
children, to avoid dishes made with nuts and nut oils. It is
also prudent to check the labels of pre-prepared ingredients
for the possible inclusion of nut derivatives.

contents

introduction

introduction

If you've picked up this book, you may already be a convert to intermittent fasting. Alternatively, you may have heard about its benefits and are wondering whether to give it a go. At the other end of the scale, you may be a battle-weary diet sceptic, still holding out a small hope that you'll one day find the way to shape up and feel healthier permanently. Whatever your starting point or motivation, and whether you have a small or large amount of weight to lose or would just like to feel more comfortable in your own skin, this is the cookbook for you.

So what is the 5:2 approach to weight loss, and how does it work? There are any number of ways in which people practise intermittent fasting, from one day of light eating a week to no food at all for several days in a row. The 5:2 approach works well for most people because it's a pragmatic solution that steers a safe, doable and yet effective path through these extremes.

How to use this book

The 5:2 plan allows normal eating for five days a week (including treats and meals out) and then restricts calorie intake to 500 calories a day for women and 600 calories a day for men (a quarter of the normal recommended daily intake) for the other two days of the week. For most people, this is the perfect compromise that allows for socializing, family life and work commitments, while still introducing enough calorie control to make sure that they lose weight at a healthy, steady rate.

With its delicious and innovative recipe selection, this book shows just how flexibly you can consume your 500 or 600 calories to keep the hunger wolf from the door and, yes, even tickle your taste buds at the same time! It also includes some sweet treats that are suitable for a fast day.

Ultimately, you'll be losing weight by eating, overall, fewer calories than your body uses

ABOUT THE RECIPES

All the recipes in this book are clearly marked with the number of calories (kcal) per serving. These figures assume that you are using low-fat versions of dairy products, so be sure to use skimmed milk and low-fat yogurt. They have also been calculated using lean meat, so make sure you trim meat of all visible fat and remove the skin from chicken breasts. Don't forget to take note of the number of portions each recipe makes and divide up the quantity of food accordingly, so that you know just how many calories you are consuming.

You'll find ideas for accompaniments and alternatives to the main recipes throughout the book – these contain the same calories or up to 20 calories more than the main recipe. However, always be careful of any additional accompaniments you may be tempted to serve with a dish, as they can be deceiving and will all contribute to your total calorie consumption.

up. But where the 5:2 diet is particularly brilliant is how marvellously achievable it can make this task for food lovers. People who find success with 5:2 often report that they failed to lose weight in the past because cutting back every day was such a struggle, whereas doing so for just a couple of days a week, albeit more drastically, is a much more attractive proposition. Better still, far from being a short-term fad, those who practise intermittent fasting find it is a lifestyle choice that they can stick to because it doesn't take over their whole lives, doesn't demonize specific foods and can even run alongside other supportive weight-loss regimens, such as online food-diary methods.

So what about the health benefits of the 5:2 diet? As you lose body fat and get trimmer, you can expect to greatly reduce your chance of having a heart attack or developing heart disease. And, in strands of research unrelated to the weight-loss benefits, there's a growing groundswell of science that shows that periodically putting your body into a fasted state may cause various chemical changes linked with a lower risk of age-related diseases and a higher chance of living healthier for longer – see pages 10–13 for more details.

Whether you're a 5:2 fan in search of healthy food inspiration, or just intrigued to know more about the diet, you'll find something in this book for you. Read, digest, get slimmer and enjoy!

Is the 5:2 diet for everyone?

Most overweight adults can benefit from a 5:2 diet, but it should never be embarked on by children or adolescents, for whom any form of nutritional stress is undesirable. Also, do not adopt the 5:2 diet if any of the following apply (check with your medical practitioner if you are uncertain):

- You are pregnant, trying to get pregnant or breastfeeding.
- You are already at the bottom end of your healthy weight. You can check this using an online Body Mass Index (BMI) calculator – a BMI of 20 or less would indicate that you are not a candidate for 5:2, or indeed any weight-loss programme.
- You are an elite athlete or in training for a marathon or other big stamina event.
- You are diabetic.
- You have irritable bowel syndrome (IBS).
- You have been diagnosed with an eating disorder, either recently or in the past.

What is intermittent fasting?

People have fasted – out of choice or through necessity – for millennia, so the general concept is far from new. Fasting for physical wellbeing and spiritual reflection is as old as the hills and all of the big religions, such as Judaism, Buddhism, Christianity and Islam, embrace fasting.

Interest was roused in the 1930s (and repeatedly since) when scientists found that restricting the calories fed to various animals and insects increased their lifespan. The idea of severely restricting calories every other day – rather than by a smaller amount every day – came later, in 2003, with laboratory research carried out at the National Institute on Aging (NIA) in the USA. The concept of intermittent fasting – and more specifically the 5:2 diet – for managing weight reached a mass audience when Dr Michael Mosley presented the theories in a programme in the BBC TV documentary series *Horizon* that was aired in August 2012.

The health benefits

There is evidence to suggest that intermittent fasting may bring health benefits over and above those offered by a conventional calorie-controlled diet.

Weight loss

When you eat 500 or 600 calories only for two days a week and don't significantly overcompensate during the remaining five days (and evidence shows that most people don't), it stands to reason that weight will start to fall off. But research indicates that

intermittent fasting may help people shed excess weight in a more efficient and effective way than normal calorie restriction.

In particular, a 2011 review by researchers at the University of Illinois, Chicago in the USA found that people who did alternate day fasting (a repeating pattern of one day unrestricted eating followed by one day of no- or low-calorie fasting) were more likely to retain higher amounts of muscle tissue while losing at least as much fat. This is important because muscle helps to keep your metabolic rate higher, in essence because it is much more metabolically active than other tissues. In short, by having a more muscular frame you can continue to burn more calories all day every day, even when you are sitting down or sleeping, which is very helpful in managing your weight over the longer term.

What doesn't kill you makes you stronger

According to Professor Mark Mattson, reported by *New Scientist* magazine to be the world's most cited neuroscientist, fasting is a type of hormesis – a process whereby organisms exposed to low levels of stress or toxins become more resistant to tougher challenges. For example, the mild biological stress induced by fasting causes cells in the heart and gut to produce proteins that decrease heart rate and blood pressure and increase gut motility (the movement of food through the gut), thereby reducing the risk of heart disease, stroke and colon cancer.

It really does seem to be a case of what doesn't kill you (i.e. managing on minimum food for a couple of days a week) makes you stronger!

Diabetes and blood sugar control

Any amount of weight loss in obese individuals, however it is achieved, will result in the body becoming more sensitive to insulin, which is an important step towards reducing the risk of diabetes – and exercise also has the effect of making you more responsive to insulin (see page 16). But intermittent fasting could have a particularly good effect on your blood sugar control and diabetes risk.

In one of Dr Michelle Harvie's studies for the UK charity Genesis Breast Cancer Prevention at Manchester's Wythenshawe Hospital, women who were on a 5:2-style intermittent fasting diet – consisting largely of milk and vegetables, adding up to 650 calories for two days each week – and a Mediterranean-style diet for the rest of the time, were compared with those who were restricted to 1,500 calories every day. In both groups women lost weight, reduced their cholesterol levels, recorded lower blood pressures and had reduced markers of breast cancer risk. When it came to reductions in fasting insulin and insulin resistance – both signs that the diabetes risk has decreased – the benefits, though modest, were greater in the 5:2 diet group than those using conventional calorie restriction.

Heart disease

As I have already alluded to, a reduction in cardiovascular risk factors, such as LDL cholesterol (that's the 'bad' type that carries cholesterol towards the arteries, where it collects and causes 'furring') and high blood pressure, can be expected on the 5:2 diet. Triglycerides in the blood will also tend to fall as you lose weight – put simply, this means that your blood is less sticky and is therefore less liable to clot.

Much of the work in this area has been done by Dr Krista Varady and her team at the University of Illinois, Chicago, with one of her scientific papers on the subject being entitled 'Intermittent fasting combined with calorie restriction is effective for weight loss and cardio-protection in obese women' (November 2012). The research carried out by Dr Varady outlines how intermittent fasting

and wider, healthy weight loss can benefit heart health. Her findings are all very much in the paper's title, really!

Brain function

Much of the research into intermittent fasting actually started, and continues, in the healthy ageing field, and brain ageing in particular. At the National Institute on Aging (NIA) in the USA they've been investigating rats and mice that have been genetically engineered to develop Alzheimer's disease. Given normal circumstances, these animals show obvious signs of dementia by the time they are a year old (for example, becoming disorientated in a maze that they have previously been able to navigate with ease), but when they're put on an on/off fasting regimen they don't develop dementia until they're around 20 months old, or much nearer the natural end of their lives.

What could be the reason? One thing that's been reported is that the fasting mouse's brain produces more of a protein called BDNF (brain-derived neurotrophic factor), which stimulates the growth of new nerve cells in the hippocampus part of the brain, essential for learning and memory. There's certainly an evolutionary logic for the fasting state to be linked with better cognitive function too: if you were hungry in caveman days, you needed your wits about you to track down the next meal and survive!

As yet there are still many unknowns, such as whether longer periods of fasting are needed than normally experienced on a 5:2 diet, and the human studies have still to be carried out, so it's impossible to say if intermittent fasting will help to prevent dementia. But it's certainly a very interesting area of research, and one to watch.

Cancer

Much of the published research into the potential disease-protective effects of intermittent fasting involve measuring a biological marker called insulin-like growth factor 1 (IGF-1), which is known to be associated with cancer. Fasting has the effect of reducing IGF-1 levels, at least temporarily, and also seems to stimulate genes that repair our body's cells.

How a reduction in IGF-1 translates into successful real-world outcomes (i.e. a reduced chance of people getting cancer) is still unclear, however. One 2007 clinical review did look at 'real-world' health outcomes and concluded that intermittent fasting (specifically, alternate day fasting, which usually has a minimum of 18-hour periods without food) may have a protective effect against cancer, as well as heart disease and diabetes. However, it concluded that 'research is required to establish definitively the consequences', which is a fair reflection of the science as it currently stands. In summary, how effective intermittent fasting is against cancer relative to other healthy-eating or weight-loss regimens is still to be clarified.

Getting started

Before you begin following your 5:2 diet, you'll need to consider some basic options and make appropriate choices to suit you and your lifestyle.

Choose your fasting days

As a first step, you'll need to decide which days will work best for you as fasting days. This may evolve over time, or from week to week, according to your circumstances. As a general rule, though, you're more likely to stick to the regimen if you can repeat the same two days every week, so try to choose days that you'll need to deviate from only infrequently. For example, don't pick a Tuesday if this is the day when a friend is most likely to invite you round for lunch, or a Friday if you're going to be tempted by a takeaway after work. For obvious reasons, weekend days may not be such good fasting days either, but everyone's different and you should choose what works for you.

The gender divide

On a fasting day:
- If you're a man, you should have no more than 600 calories.
- If you're a woman, you should have no more than 500 calories.
- It is a fact that, even if a man and a woman weigh the same, the man will usually burn more calories than the woman because he has a higher proportion of muscle (see page 11).

Fast day meals

The second decision to make is how you will spread your 500 or 600 calories over the fasting day. Again, this is down to personal preference, usually honed through trial and error. A satisfying format for many people is to bookend their day with two meals – a 100–200-calorie breakfast and a 300-calorie dinner, for example, with the possibility of 100 calories or so for snacking or another small meal in between if desired. Other people report that they are happier if they don't eat their first morsel until brunch or lunch, while still others (usually men, on anecdotal evidence) prefer saving up their calories for just one reasonable-sized meal – either a lunch or an evening meal.

Six top tips for beginners

1 The day before your first fast, eat well and aim to go to bed feeling neither hungry nor overfull. Getting an early night is good preparation. Trying to stuff in as much food as late as possible so that you don't feel hungry tomorrow is not!

2 Do your eating homework so that you know how you are going to spend your 500 or 600 calories, and which meals you are going to spread them between. Use the recipes in this book as inspiration, and make sure that you are stocked up with the requisite ingredients.

3 Try to make your environment as devoid of food temptations as possible, which means ensuring that a stray slice of pork pie isn't the first thing screaming, 'eat me!' when you open the fridge door.

4 Arm yourself with some kind of calorie counter – use an online app or website.

5 Be aware that choosing a less busy day to start your fasting may not be the best approach. As long as you have your food choices pre-planned, a day with plenty to keep you occupied may be better.

6 If you find your first fast too hard and have to give in, you've probably just chosen the wrong day. Don't despair and try again another time, but leave it a few days before doing so.

Fast day eating

Theoretically, you could have a large burger and endless cups of black coffee on a fast day and be within your calorie allowance, but this wouldn't be good for you. Instead, use your fasting day to make balanced and healthy choices, using the following guidelines:

• Eat five a day – fill up on fruit and veg
• Include dairy and pulses
• Include lean protein
• Choose quality carbs
• Choose calorie-free drink options
• Don't estimate

Perfect fast day proportions

– **Concentrate on fruit and vegetables** (steamed, grilled, stir-fried or in soups, smoothies and salads) as your primary stomach-filling priority (up to 200 calories).

– **Most of the remaining calories** (300 or 400) will be best spent on low-GI, carbohydrate-rich and/or protein-rich foods.

– **Any calories left over** you can use as you wish (see below for ideas), but choosing more highly nutritious foods is preferable.

Give yourself a treat

– **Snacks up to 50 calories** include 100 g (3½ oz) cherry tomatoes, 1 oatcake spread with yeast extract or a sachet of miso soup with tofu.

– **Snacks up to 100 calories** include 1 medium apple or banana, 15 g (½ oz) plain almonds, 1 digestive biscuit or 1 hard-boiled egg.

'Off' day eating

Does all this mean you can truly eat anything you want to on your five free days? Well, yes, but there are limits. Studies consistently show that, contrary to what you might expect, intermittent fasters are actually very unlikely to go on big binges on their 'off' days. Rather than make your appetite more extreme, the 5:2 dieting seems to help naturally regulate it so that you enjoy only as much food as you need when you aren't fasting.

Exercise and 5:2

An exercise programme can definitely complement your 5:2 weight-loss progress, and will provide many attendant health benefits, such as stronger bones and a healthier heart. But how should you negotiate exercise on a fast day? The old wisdom was that you should be well fuelled prior to exercise, but the latest evidence suggests that modest activity in the fasted state is actually good for you. In particular, exercising in the fasted state means that the body has to use fat as its primary fuel, which is good news for the disappearance of those love handles! Another benefit of exercising on an empty stomach appears to be that you'll build muscle more effectively when you do get round to eating in the post-exercise period.

In a nutshell, there's no reason why you shouldn't work out on your fast day, with the ideal being to exercise when you are feeling hungry, perhaps in the afternoon, and then to follow with one of your fast day meals. However, common sense must come into play and if you're new to exercise it's best to ease yourself into physical activity on non-fast days only. There's also some suggestion that women are better doing weights on fasting days, while men can particularly benefit from cardio work. Listening to your body is essential, and you should always stop exercising immediately if you feel faint, dizzy or light-headed.

How active should I be?

Official guidelines suggest that for optimum health benefits you should be physically active (at the level of brisk walking or gentle cycling, for example) for at least 30 minutes five times a week. If you're doing something more vigorous, such as running or playing a racquet sport, you can get away with 75 minutes, or three 25-minute sessions a week. On top of this, one or two 20-minute sessions with weights are also recommended to maintain muscle tone and lean tissue levels, particularly in the over 40s.

5:2 for life

For now, the consensus approach from most people doing 5:2 who have already reached their ideal weight and don't wish to become any slimmer is to switch to 500- or 600-calorie fasting just one day a week (a 6:1 diet!). A small study showed that people who had lost weight could keep it off by doing this, though another approach, if you want to maintain a slightly firmer watch on your weight, would be to continue with two fast days a week, but let them creep up to, say, 700 calories.

Some people may find that they can manage by using 5:2 fasting now and again (intermittent intermittent fasting, if you like!), or to stop for longer periods or even altogether. These folk will be the ones who have become confident in their own eating intuition to keep them safe from weight gain. In short, they can now trust their inbuilt hunger and fullness mechanisms (that were, in fact, there all the time) to stay happily at their optimum weight.

Whatever your approach, remember that you should always obtain pleasure from your eating and your diet should never become a terrible chore. If you choose intermittent fasting as your ongoing method of optimizing health and weight, the recipes that follow should make that eminently possible, for as long as you choose.

breakfasts & brunches

fruity summer milkshake

Calories per serving **89**
Makes **2 x 300 ml** (½ **pint)**
  glasses
Preparation time **2 minutes**

1 ripe **peach**, halved, stoned
  and chopped
150 g (5 oz) **strawberries**
150 g (5 oz) **raspberries**
200 ml (7 fl oz) **skimmed milk**
ice cubes

Put the peach in a blender or food processor with the strawberries and raspberries and blend to a smooth purée, scraping the mixture down from the sides of the bowl if necessary.

Add the milk and blend the ingredients again until the mixture is smooth and frothy. Pour the milkshake over the ice cubes in 2 tall glasses.

For soya milk & mango shake, replace the peach, strawberries and raspberries with ½ large ripe mango and the juice of 1 orange. Purée as above, then pour in 200 ml (7 fl oz) light soya milk, blend and serve over ice cubes as above.

maple-glazed granola with fruit

Calories per serving **246**
Serves **6**
Preparation time **20 minutes**,
  plus cooling
Cooking time **7–10 minutes**

2 tablespoons **olive oil**
2 tablespoons **maple syrup**
40 g (1½ oz) **flaked almonds**
40 g (1½ oz) **pine nuts**
25 g (1 oz) **sunflower seeds**
25 g (1 oz) **porridge oats**
375 ml (12 fl oz) **low-fat
  natural yogurt**

Fruit salad
1 **mango**, stoned, peeled
  and sliced
2 **kiwifruit**, peeled and sliced
1 small bunch of **red seedless
  grapes**, halved
grated rind and juice of **1 lime**

Heat the oil in a flameproof frying pan with a metal
handle, add the maple syrup and the nuts, seeds and
oats and toss together.

Transfer the pan to a preheated oven, 180°C (350°F),
Gas Mark 4, and cook for 5–8 minutes, stirring once
and moving the brown edges to the centre, until the
granola mixture is evenly toasted.

Leave the mixture to cool, then pack it into a storage jar,
seal, label and consume within 10 days.

Make the fruit salad. Mix the fruits with the lime rind
and juice, spoon the mixture into 6 dishes and top with
spoonfuls of natural yogurt and granola.

For berry compote, to serve with the granola
instead of the fruit salad, place 150 g (5 oz) each of
raspberries, blackberries and blueberries in a pan with
the grated rind and juice of 1 lemon. Heat gently until
the fruit has softened and the blueberries burst, then
sweeten with 1 teaspoon honey. Serve with the granola
and yogurt as above.

moroccan baked eggs

Calories per serving **170**
Serves **2**
Preparation time **10 minutes**
Cooking time **25–35 minutes**

½ tablespoon **olive oil**
½ **onion**, chopped
1 **garlic clove**, sliced
½ teaspoon **ras el hanout**
pinch of **ground cinnamon**
½ teaspoon **ground coriander**
400 g (13 oz) **cherry
  tomatoes**
2 tablespoons chopped
  coriander
2 **eggs**
salt and **pepper**

Heat the oil in a frying pan, add the onion and garlic and cook for 6–7 minutes until softened and lightly golden. Stir in the spices and cook, stirring, for a further 1 minute.

Add the tomatoes and season well with salt and pepper, then simmer gently for 8–10 minutes.

Scatter over 1 tablespoon of the coriander, then divide the tomato mixture between 2 individual ovenproof dishes. Break an egg into each dish.

Bake in a preheated oven, 220°C (425°F), Gas Mark 7, for 8–10 minutes until the egg whites are set but the yolks are still slightly runny. Cook for a further 2–3 minutes if you prefer the eggs to be cooked through. Serve scattered with the remaining coriander.

For Mexican baked eggs, heat 1 tablespoon olive oil in a frying pan, add 1 chopped onion and 1 cored, deseeded and chopped red pepper and cook until softened. Add 2 crushed garlic cloves and ½ teaspoon chilli powder and cook, stirring, for a further 1 minute. Stir in a 400 g (13 oz) can chopped tomatoes and simmer gently for 8–10 minutes, then add 1 tablespoon chopped coriander. Divide between 2 individual ovenproof dishes and break an egg into each, then bake as above. Serve with 1 stoned, peeled and sliced avocado, if liked.

cranberry muffins

Calories per muffin **172**
Makes **12**
Preparation time **10 minutes**
Cooking time **18–20 minutes**

150 g (5 oz) **plain flour**
150 g (5 oz) **self-raising flour**
1 tablespoon **baking powder**
65 g (2½ oz) **light**
   muscovado sugar
3 pieces of **stem ginger** from
   a jar, about 50 g (2 oz),
   finely chopped
100 g (3½ oz) **dried**
   cranberries
1 **egg**
250 ml (8 fl oz) **skimmed milk**
4 tablespoons **vegetable oil**

Line a 12-hole muffin tin with paper muffin cases. Sift the flours and baking powder into a large bowl. Stir in the sugar, ginger and cranberries until evenly distributed.

Beat together the egg, milk and oil in a separate bowl, then add the liquid to the flour mixture. Using a large metal spoon, gently stir the liquid into the flour until only just combined. The mixture should look craggy, with specks of flour still visible.

Divide the mixture between the muffin cases, piling it up in the centre. Bake in a preheated oven, 200°C (400°F), Gas Mark 6, for 18–20 minutes until well risen and golden. Transfer to a wire rack and serve while still slightly warm.

For wholemeal apricot & orange muffins, replace the plain flour with 150 g (5 oz) wholemeal flour. Use 100 g (3½ oz) chopped dried apricots instead of the cranberries and omit the ginger. Fold the finely grated rind of 1 orange into the mixture before baking.

breakfast cereal bars

Calories per bar **156**
Makes **16**
Preparation time **10 minutes**,
  plus cooling
Cooking time **35 minutes**

100 g (3½ oz) **butter**,
  softened
25 g (1 oz) **light muscovado
  sugar**
2 tablespoons **golden syrup**
125 g (4 oz) **millet flakes**
50 g (2 oz) **quinoa**
50 g (2 oz) **dried cherries** or
  cranberries
75 g (3 oz) **sultanas**
25 g (1 oz) **sunflower seeds**
25 g (1 oz) **sesame seeds**
25 g (1 oz) **linseeds**
40 g (1½ oz) **unsweetened
  desiccated coconut**
2 **eggs**, lightly beaten

Grease a 28 x 20 cm (11 x 8 inch) shallow rectangular baking tin. Beat together the butter, sugar and syrup in a bowl until creamy.

Add all the remaining ingredients and beat well until combined. Turn into the prepared tin and level the surface with the back of a dessertspoon.

Bake in a preheated oven, 180°C (350°F), Gas Mark 4, for 35 minutes until deep golden. Leave to cool in the tin.

Turn out on to a wooden board and carefully cut into 16 fingers using a serrated knife.

For tropical cereal bars, prepare the recipe as above, replacing the dried cherries or cranberries with 50 g (2 oz) finely chopped dried pineapple and replacing the sultanas with 75 g (3 oz) dried mango.

vanilla muffins

Calories per muffin **198**
Makes **12**
Preparation time **10 minutes**,
   plus cooling
Cooking time **25 minutes**

1 **vanilla pod**
200 ml (7 fl oz) **skimmed milk**
325 g (11 oz) **self-raising
   flour**
1 tablespoon **baking powder**
125 g (4 oz) **caster sugar**
2 **eggs**
4 tablespoons **vegetable oil**
200 ml (7 fl oz) **low-fat
   natural yogurt**
icing sugar, for dusting

Line a 12-hole muffin tin with squares of greaseproof paper. Split the vanilla pod lengthways, using the tip of a sharp knife, and place in a small saucepan with 100 ml (3½ fl oz) of the milk. Bring just to the boil, then remove from the heat and leave to cool slightly. Remove the vanilla pod from the pan and scoop out the seeds with a teaspoon. Stir them into the milk and discard the pod.

Sift the flour and baking powder into a large bowl, then stir in the sugar. In a separate bowl, beat together the eggs, vegetable oil, yogurt, vanilla milk and remaining milk. Using a large metal spoon, gently stir the liquid into the flour until only just combined.

Spoon the mixture into the muffin cases and bake in a preheated oven, 200°C (400°F), Gas Mark 6, for about 20 minutes until well risen and golden. Transfer to a wire rack and dust with icing sugar. Serve slightly warm.

For cinnamon muffins, infuse the milk with vanilla as above, also adding 1 cinnamon stick. Let the milk cool completely before removing the cinnamon stick and vanilla pod. Make the muffin mixture as above and spoon into the muffin cases. Combine 1 tablespoon golden granulated sugar and 1 teaspoon ground cinnamon and lightly sprinkle over the mixture, then bake as above.

light 'n' low pancakes

Calories per serving **194**
Serves **4**
Preparation time **5 minutes**,
   plus standing
Cooking time **25 minutes**

125 g (4 oz) **brown** or
   wholemeal plain flour
1 **egg**
300 ml (½ pint) **skimmed
   milk** (if using wholemeal flour
   you will need a little more)
1 teaspoon **vegetable oil**, plus
   a little extra for cooking

Topping
mixed fresh berries
125 g (4 oz) **low-fat (less
   than 3%) crème fraîche**

Sift the flour into a bowl. If using wholemeal flour, also add the bran in the sieve to the flour in the bowl.

Beat together the egg, milk and oil in a separate bowl, then slowly add to the flour. Stir the mixture until a smooth batter forms. Leave to stand for about 20 minutes, then stir again.

Heat a little oil in a nonstick frying pan, or spray with an oil-water spray. When the oil is hot, add 2 tablespoons of the pancake mixture and shake the pan so that it spreads. Cook for 2 minutes until the underside is lightly browned, then flip or turn the pancake over and cook the other side for a minute or so.

Keep the pancake warm in the oven while you cook the rest – you can stack one on top of the other as they are cooked. The mixture should make 8 pancakes in total. Serve 2 pancakes per person topped with a handful of mixed fresh berries and a dollop of crème fraîche.

For strawberry & lime crush, to serve with the pancakes, blend the grated rind and juice of 1 lime with 150 g (5 oz) strawberries and 2 teaspoons honey in a bowl until it forms a coarse purée. Adjust the sweetness to taste and serve with the pancakes.

piperade with pastrami

Calories per serving **186**
Serves **6**
Preparation time **20 minutes**,
    plus cooling
Cooking time **25 minutes**

6 large **eggs**
thyme sprigs, leaves removed,
    or large pinch of **dried**
    thyme, plus extra sprigs
    to garnish
1 tablespoon **olive oil**
125 g (4 oz) **pastrami**,
    thinly sliced
salt and **pepper**

Sofrito
375 g (12 oz), or 3 small,
    different coloured **peppers**
1 tablespoon **olive oil**
1 **onion**, finely chopped
2 **garlic cloves**, crushed
500 g (1 lb) **tomatoes**,
    skinned (see page 162),
    deseeded and chopped

Make the sofrito. Grill or cook the peppers directly
in a gas flame for about 10 minutes, turning them until
the skins have blistered and blackened. Remove the
peppers and place them in a plastic bag. Seal and leave
to cool for 20 minutes, then rub the skins from the flesh
and discard. Rinse the peppers under cold running
water. Halve and deseed, then cut the flesh into strips.

Heat the oil in a large frying pan, add the onion
and cook gently for 10 minutes until softened and
transparent. Add the garlic, tomatoes and peppers and
simmer for 5 minutes until any juice has evaporated
from the tomatoes. Set aside until ready to serve.

Beat the eggs with the thyme and salt and pepper in
a bowl. Reheat the sofrito. Heat the oil in a saucepan,
add the eggs, stirring until they are lightly scrambled.
Stir into the reheated sofrito and spoon on to 6 plates.

Arrange slices of pastrami around the eggs and serve
immediately, garnished with a little extra thyme.

For poached egg piperade, make the sofrito as above.
Place 300 g (10 oz) washed baby spinach leaves in
a large saucepan, cover and cook briefly just until the
leaves start to wilt. Divide between 6 serving plates, then
spoon over the sofrito. Poach the 6 eggs (see page 106)
instead of scrambling them, then sit them on top. Dust
each egg with a tiny pinch of paprika and serve, omitting
the pastrami.

corn & bacon muffins

Calories per muffin **228**
Makes **12**
Preparation time **10 minutes**
Cooking time **20–25 minutes**

6 **streaky bacon rashers**,
  excess fat removed,
  finely chopped
1 small **red onion**, finely
  chopped
200 g (7 oz) **frozen**
  sweetcorn
175 g (6 oz) **fine cornmeal**
125 g (4 oz) **plain flour**
2 teaspoons **baking powder**
50 g (2 oz) **Cheddar cheese**,
  grated
200 ml (7 fl oz) **skimmed milk**
2 **eggs**
3 tablespoons **vegetable oil**

Lightly oil a 12-hole muffin tin.

Dry-fry the bacon and onion in a nonstick frying pan over a medium heat for 3–4 minutes until the bacon is turning crisp. Meanwhile, cook the sweetcorn in a saucepan of boiling water for 2 minutes to soften. Drain.

Put the cornmeal, flour and baking powder in a bowl and mix together. Add the sweetcorn, cheese, bacon and onions, then stir in.

Whisk the milk with the eggs and oil in a separate bowl, then add to the dry ingredients. Stir gently until just combined, then divide the mixture between the muffin tin sections.

Bake in a preheated oven, 220°C (425°F), Gas Mark 7, for 15–20 minutes until golden and just firm. Loosen the edges of the muffins with a knife and transfer to a wire rack to cool.

For spiced corn & spring onion muffins, omit the bacon. Prepare the recipe as above, replacing the red onion with 4 spring onions, sliced thinly into rounds. Add 1 teaspoon hot paprika and 1 deseeded and finely chopped red chilli to the mixture before baking as above.

potato drop scones

Calories per scone **68**
Makes **12**
Preparation time **10 minutes**,
   plus cooling
Cooking time **20–25 minutes**

550 g (1 lb 2 oz) large
   potatoes, peeled and cut
   into small chunks
1½ teaspoons **baking powder**
2 **eggs**
75 ml (3 fl oz) **skimmed milk**
vegetable oil, for frying
salt and **pepper**

Cook the potatoes in a saucepan of lightly salted boiling water for 15 minutes or until completely tender. Drain well, return to the saucepan and mash until smooth. Leave to cool slightly.

Beat in the baking powder, then the eggs, milk and a little seasoning, and continue to beat until everything is evenly combined.

Heat a little oil in a heavy-based frying pan. Drop heaped dessertspoonfuls of the mixture into the pan, spacing them slightly apart, and fry for 3–4 minutes, turning once, until golden.

Transfer to a serving plate and keep warm while frying the remainder of the potato mixture to make 12 scones. (If grilling the potato scones, put 12 heaped dessertspoonfuls of the mixture on an oiled, foil-lined baking sheet and cook under a preheated grill for 5 minutes, turning once halfway through the cooking time.) Serve warm, drizzled with maple syrup and accompanied by grilled tomatoes and lean bacon rashers, if liked (remembering to count the extra calories).

For mustard potato & green bean drop scones, prepare the mixture as above, adding 75 g (3 oz) finely sliced blanched green beans and 1 tablespoon wholegrain mustard before cooking as above.

asparagus with smoked salmon

Calories per serving **150**
Serves **6**
Preparation time **10 minutes**
Cooking time **6 minutes**

200 g (7 oz) trimmed
  asparagus
3 tablespoons roughly
  chopped **hazelnuts**
4 teaspoons **olive oil**
juice of **1 lime**
1 teaspoon **Dijon mustard**
12 **quail eggs**
250 g (8 oz) **smoked salmon**
salt and **pepper**

Put the asparagus spears in a steamer, cover and cook for 5 minutes until just tender.

Meanwhile, grill the nuts on a piece of foil until lightly browned. Lightly mix together the oil, lime juice and mustard with a little salt and pepper in a bowl, then stir in the hot nuts. Keep warm.

Pour water into a saucepan to a depth of 4 cm (1 ½ inches) and bring it to the boil. Lower the eggs into the water with a slotted spoon and cook for 1 minute. Take the pan off the heat and leave the eggs to stand for 1 minute. Drain the eggs, rinse with cold water and drain again.

Tear the salmon into strips and divide it between 6 serving plates, folding and twisting the strips attractively. Tuck the just-cooked asparagus into the salmon, halve the quail eggs, leaving the shells on if liked, and arrange on top. Drizzle with the warm nut dressing and serve sprinkled with a little black pepper.

For asparagus with Parma ham & ricotta, steam the asparagus and make the dressing as above. Remove the fat from 12 slices of Parma ham, then divide the slices between 6 plates, so each has 2 slices, and spoon 2 tablespoons ricotta into the centre of each plate. Arrange the asparagus around the ricotta and drizzle with the dressing. Omit the quail eggs and smoked salmon.

courgette & stilton fritters

Calories per fritter **95**
Makes **20**
Preparation time **10 minutes**
Cooking time **10 minutes**

1 tablespoon **olive oil**
1 large **courgette**, chopped
3 **eggs**
150 ml (¼ pint) **skimmed milk**
150 g (5 oz) **self-raising
   flour**, sifted
400 g (13 oz) can **flageolet
   beans**, drained and rinsed
handful of **parsley**, chopped
3 **spring onions**, sliced
325 g (11 oz) can **sweetcorn
   kernels**, drained
100 g (3½ oz) **Stilton cheese**,
   crumbled

Heat a little of the oil in a nonstick frying pan, add
the courgette and fry for 3–4 minutes until golden
and tender.

Beat together the eggs, milk and flour in a bowl, then
stir in the beans, parsley, spring onions, sweetcorn,
Stilton and the cooked courgette.

Heat the remaining oil in a nonstick frying pan and
add tablespoons of the mixture to the pan. Gently
flatten each fritter with the back of a fork and fry for
1–2 minutes on each side until golden. Repeat with
the remaining mixture to make 20 fritters, keeping
the fritters warm in a low oven.

Serve with tomato salsa, if liked (remembering to
count the extra calories).

For spinach & Stilton fritters, replace the courgettes
with 200 g (7 oz) baby spinach leaves. Cook in a
nonstick frying pan with a little oil for 1–2 minutes
until wilted, then stir in the remaining ingredients,
replacing the flageolet beans with a 400 g (13 oz) can
of cannellini beans, and also adding a large pinch of
freshly grated nutmeg. Cook and serve as above.

olive & sun-dried tomato scones

Calories per scone **198**
Makes **8**
Preparation time **15 minutes**
Cooking time **12 minutes**

175 g (6 oz) **rice flour**
75 g (3 oz) **potato flour**
1 teaspoon **xanthan gum**
1 teaspoon **baking powder**
1 teaspoon **bicarbonate
of soda**
75 g (3 oz) **butter**, cubed
25 g (1 oz) **pitted green
olives**, chopped
4 **sun-dried tomatoes**,
chopped
1 tablespoon chopped **parsley**
1 large **egg**, beaten
4 tablespoons **buttermilk**, plus
a little extra for brushing

Place the flours, xanthan gum, baking powder, bicarbonate of soda and butter in a food processor and whiz until the mixture resembles fine breadcrumbs, or rub in by hand in a large bowl.

Stir the olives, tomatoes and parsley into the mixture, then, using the blade of a knife, stir in the egg and buttermilk until the mixture comes together.

Tip the dough out on to a surface dusted lightly with flour and gently press it down to a thickness of 2.5 cm (1 inch). Use a 5 cm (2 inch) cutter to cut out 8 scones.

Place on a lightly floured baking sheet, brush with a little buttermilk and bake in a preheated oven, 220°C (425°F), Gas Mark 7, for about 12 minutes until golden and risen. Transfer to a wire rack to cool.

For ham & cheese scones, prepare the mixture as above, replacing the green olives with 25 g (1 oz) roughly chopped honey roast ham. Add 2 tablespoons grated Parmesan cheese to the mixture before working in the egg and buttermilk. Continue as above.

light lunches

lentil & pea soup

Calories per serving **141**
Serves **4**
Preparation time **10 minutes**
Cooking time **2 hours**

1 teaspoon **olive oil**
1 **leek**, trimmed and finely sliced
1 **garlic clove**, crushed
400 g (13 oz) can **Puy
  lentils**, drained
2 tablespoons chopped
  mixed herbs, such as thyme
  and parsley
200 g (7 oz) **frozen peas**
2 tablespoons **low-fat (less
  than 3%) crème fraîche**
1 tablespoon chopped **mint**
pepper

Vegetable stock
1 tablespoon **olive oil**
1 **onion**, chopped
1 **carrot**, chopped
4 **celery sticks**, chopped
any **vegetable trimmings**,
  such as celery tops, onion
  skins and tomato skins
1 **bouquet garni**
1.3 litres (2¼ pints) **water**
salt and **pepper**

Make the stock. Heat the oil in a large saucepan,
add the vegetables and fry for 2–3 minutes, then
add the vegetable trimmings and bouquet garni and
season well. Pour over the measurement water and
bring to the boil, then reduce the heat and simmer
gently for 1½ hours, by which time the stock should
have reduced to 900 ml (1½ pints). Drain over a bowl,
discarding the vegetables and retaining the stock.

Heat the oil in a medium saucepan, add the leek and
garlic and fry over a gentle heat for 5–6 minutes until
the leek is softened.

Add the lentils, stock and herbs and bring to the boil,
then reduce the heat and simmer for 10 minutes. Add
the peas and cook for a further 5 minutes until tender.

Transfer half the soup to a blender or food processor
and blend until smooth. Return to the pan, stir to
combine with the unblended soup, then heat through
and season with plenty of pepper.

Ladle the soup into 4 bowls. Stir together the crème
fraîche and mint and serve alongside each bowl of soup.

For curried lentil & parsnip soup, make the stock
as above. Heat the olive oil in a saucepan, add the
leek and garlic with 2 chopped parsnips and cook
for 5–6 minutes until the vegetables are softened.
Add 1 teaspoon curry powder and cook, stirring, for
1 minute. Continue as above, omitting the peas.

chilled gazpacho

Calories per serving **135**
Serves **6**
Preparation time **20 minutes**,
    plus chilling

875 g (1¾ lb) **tomatoes**,
    skinned (see page 162)
    and roughly chopped
½ **cucumber**, roughly chopped
2 **red peppers**, cored,
    deseeded and roughly
    chopped
1 **celery stick**, chopped
2 **garlic cloves**, chopped
½ **red chilli**, deseeded
    and sliced
small handful of **coriander** or
    flat leaf parsley, plus extra
    to garnish
2 tablespoons **white wine
    vinegar**
2 tablespoons **sun-dried
    tomato paste**
4 tablespoons **olive oil**
salt

To serve
ice cubes
hard-boiled egg, finely
    chopped
a little **cucumber, pepper** and
    onion, finely chopped

Mix together the vegetables, garlic, chilli and coriander
or parsley in a large bowl.

Add the vinegar, tomato paste, oil and a little salt.
Process in batches in a food processor or blender until
smooth, scraping the mixture down from the sides of
the bowl if necessary.

Collect the blended mixtures together in a clean bowl
and check the seasoning, adding a little more salt if
needed. Chill for up to 24 hours before serving.

Ladle the gazpacho into 6 large bowls, scatter with ice
cubes and garnish with chopped parsley or coriander
and a little chopped hard-boiled egg, cucumber, pepper
and onion. Serve with crackers, if liked (remembering
to count the extra calories).

For chilled couscous gazpacho, prepare the soup
as above, omitting the red peppers, and chill. Place
45 g (1¾ oz) couscous in a bowl and pour in just
enough boiling water to come 1 cm (½ in) above the
level of the couscous. Cover with clingfilm and set aside
for 10 minutes. Uncover, break the couscous up with a
fork and leave to cool to room temperature. Stir into the
soup just before serving with the chopped herbs and a
little harissa on the side. Omit the ice and garnishes.

sweet potato & cabbage soup

Calories per serving **160**
Serves **4**
Preparation time **15 minutes**
Cooking time **25 minutes**

2 **onions**, chopped
2 **garlic cloves**, sliced
4 **lean back bacon rashers**,
  chopped
500 g (1 lb) **sweet potatoes**,
  peeled and chopped
2 **parsnips**, peeled and
  chopped
1 teaspoon chopped **thyme**
900 ml (1 ½ pints) **Vegetable
  Stock** (see page 48)
1 **baby Savoy cabbage**,
  shredded

Place the onions, garlic and bacon in a large saucepan
and fry for 2–3 minutes.

Add the sweet potatoes, parsnips, thyme and stock and
bring to the boil, then reduce the heat and simmer for
15 minutes.

Transfer two-thirds of the soup to a blender or food
processor and blend until smooth. Return the soup to
the pan, add the cabbage and simmer for a further
5–7 minutes until the cabbage is just cooked.

Ladle the soup into 4 bowls and serve immediately.

For squash & broccoli soup, make the recipe as
above, replacing the sweet potatoes with 500 g (1 lb)
peeled, deseeded and chopped butternut squash. After
returning the blended soup to the pan, add 100 g
(3½ oz) broccoli, broken into small florets. Cook as
above, omitting the cabbage.

bacon & white bean soup

Calories per serving **136**
Serves **4**
Preparation time **5 minutes**
Cooking time **15 minutes**

1 teaspoon **olive oil**
2 **lean smoked bacon rashers**, chopped
2 **garlic cloves**, crushed
1 **onion**, chopped
a few **thyme** or **lemon thyme sprigs**
2 x 400 g (13 oz) cans **cannellini beans**, drained and rinsed
900 ml (1½ pints) **Vegetable Stock** (see page 48)
2 tablespoons chopped **parsley**
pepper

Heat the oil in a large saucepan, add the bacon, garlic and onion and fry for 3–4 minutes until the bacon is beginning to brown and the onion to soften.

Add the thyme and fry for a further 1 minute. Add the beans and stock to the pan and bring to the boil, then reduce the heat and simmer for 10 minutes.

Transfer the soup to a blender or food processor and blend with the parsley and pepper until smooth.

Return the soup to the pan and heat through, then ladle into 4 bowls and serve immediately.

For herb & white bean crostini, lightly mash a drained 400 g (13 oz) can cannellini beans and then combine with 2 tablespoons each of finely chopped basil and parsley, 1 crushed garlic clove, a pinch of dried chilli flakes and 50 g (2 oz) chopped cherry tomatoes. Toast 8 thin slices of baguette and top with the herby bean mixture.

miso broth with prawns

Calories per serving **57**
Serves **6**
Preparation time **10 minutes**
Cooking time **12–13 minutes**

4 **spring onions** or **baby
 leeks**, thinly sliced
1.5 cm (¾ inch) piece of **fresh
 root ginger**, peeled and
 finely chopped
½–1 large **red chilli**,
 deseeded and thinly sliced
1.5 litres (2½ pints) **fish
 or Vegetable Stock**
 (see page 48)
3 tablespoons **chilled miso**
2 tablespoons **mirin** (Japanese
 cooking wine)
1 tablespoon **soy sauce**
100 g (3½ oz) **pak choi**,
 thinly sliced
2 tablespoons chopped
 coriander
150 g (5 oz) **frozen cooked
 peeled prawns**, thawed
 and rinsed

Put the white parts of the spring onions or leeks into
a saucepan with the ginger, sliced chilli and stock.

Add the miso, mirin and soy sauce, stir and bring to the
boil, then reduce the heat and simmer for 5 minutes.

Stir in the green parts of the spring onions or leeks, the
pak choi, coriander and prawns and cook together for
2–3 minutes or until the pak choi has just wilted. Ladle
into 6 bowls and serve.

For vegetarian miso broth, prepare the soup as above.
When adding the pak choi, also stir in 1 large carrot, cut
into matchsticks, and 50 g (2 oz) bean sprouts. Cook as
above for 2–3 minutes. Omit the prawns.

sautéed kidneys with marsala

Calories per serving **303**
Serves **6**
Preparation time **20 minutes**
Cooking time **20–25 minutes**

15 g (½ oz) **butter**
1 tablespoon **olive oil**
1 **onion**, thinly sliced
10 **lambs' kidneys**, cored
   and trimmed
375 g (12 oz) **cherry**
   tomatoes, halved
1 teaspoon **Dijon mustard**
1 teaspoon **tomato purée**
200 ml (7 fl oz) **Marsala**
8 **streaky bacon rashers**,
   excess fat removed
50 g (2 oz) **wild rocket leaves**
4 teaspoons **balsamic vinegar**
3 slices of **wholegrain bread**
salt and **pepper**

Heat the butter and oil in a frying pan, add the onion and cook for 5 minutes until softened and lightly browned. Add the kidneys and fry over a high heat for 3 minutes until browned.

Add the tomatoes and cook for 2 minutes, then stir in the mustard, tomato purée, Marsala and salt and pepper. Cook for 2–3 minutes, stirring, until the sauce has reduced slightly and the kidneys are cooked. Cover with a lid and keep hot.

Meanwhile, wind the bacon around 8 metal skewers and cook under a preheated hot grill for 8–10 minutes until crisp. Toss the rocket leaves in the vinegar. Toast the bread and cut each slice in half.

Arrange the toast on 6 serving plates and spoon the the kidneys on to the toast. Slide the skewers from the bacon and arrange the bacon attractively on the kidneys. Spoon the rocket salad on the side and serve immediately.

For beef strips with Marsala, replace the kidneys with 500 g (1 lb) lean beef steak, cut into thin strips. Cook the beef with the ingredients up to and including the Marsala as above, then remove from the heat and stir in the rocket, balsamic vinegar and 50 g (2 oz) toasted pine nuts. Set aside for the rocket to wilt. Omit the bacon and toast, and serve.

peppered beef with salad leaves

Calories per serving **148**
Serves **6**
Preparation time **20 minutes**
Cooking time **4–7 minutes**

2 **thick-cut sirloin steaks**,
about 500 g (1 lb) in total,
trimmed of fat
3 teaspoons **coloured
peppercorns**, coarsely
crushed
coarse salt flakes
200 ml (7 fl oz) **low-fat
natural yogurt**
1–1½ teaspoons **horseradish
sauce** (to taste)
1 **garlic clove**, crushed
150 g (5 oz) **mixed green
salad leaves**
100 g (3½ oz) **button
mushrooms**, sliced
1 **red onion**, thinly sliced
1 tablespoon **olive oil**
salt and **pepper**

Rub the steaks with the crushed peppercorns and salt.

Mix together the yogurt, horseradish sauce and garlic
in a bowl and season to taste with salt and pepper. Add
the salad leaves, mushrooms and most of the red onion
and toss gently.

Heat the oil in a frying pan, add the steaks and cook
over a high heat for 2 minutes until browned. Turn over
and cook for a further 2 minutes for medium rare,
3–4 minutes for medium or 5 minutes for well done.

Spoon the salad leaves into the centre of 6 serving
plates. Thinly slice the steaks and arrange the pieces
on top, then garnish with the remaining red onion.

For lemon beef with mustard dressing, trim the
steaks and season with salt and a light grinding of black
pepper. Make the salad as above, replacing the yogurt
with 200 g (7 oz) low-fat (less than 3%) crème fraîche
and using 2 tablespoons wholegrain mustard instead of
the horseradish. Cook the steaks as above, adding the
juice of ½ lemon to the frying pan after removing the
steaks from the heat. Turn the steaks in the lemon
a couple of times, then serve as above.

lentil & goats' cheese salad

Calories per serving **250**
Serves **2**
Preparation time **15 minutes**
Cooking time **20–25 minutes**

1 teaspoon **olive oil**
1 teaspoon **cumin seeds**
1 **garlic clove**, crushed
1 teaspoon peeled and grated
  fresh root ginger
50 g (2 oz) **Puy lentils**,
  well rinsed
375 ml (13 fl oz) hot **chicken**
  or **Vegetable Stock**
  (see page 48)
1 tablespoon chopped **mint**
1 tablespoon chopped
  coriander
squeeze of **lime juice**
75 g (3 oz) **baby spinach**
  leaves
50 g (2 oz) **goats' cheese**,
  crumbled
pepper

Heat the oil in a saucepan, add the cumin seeds, garlic and ginger and cook, stirring, for 1 minute. Add the lentils and cook for a further 1 minute.

Add the hot stock to the pan one ladleful at a time, allowing the liquid to be absorbed before adding more, and cook until the lentils are tender – 15–20 minutes. Remove the pan from the heat and stir in the herbs and lime juice.

Divide the spinach leaves between 2 serving bowls, top with the lentils and goats' cheese and sprinkle with black pepper.

For lentil & goats' cheese soup, cook the cumin seeds, garlic and ginger in the oil as above, then add a drained 400 g (13 oz) can Puy lentils and 600 ml (1 pint) hot vegetable stock and simmer for 10 minutes. Stir in the herbs and lime juice. Blend the soup with a hand blender until smooth, adding a little more stock if needed, or transfer to a blender or food processor. Return to the pan and reheat gently, if necessary. Stir through 2 tablespoons low-fat natural yogurt, season to taste with salt and pepper and serve sprinkled with the crumbled goats' cheese.

chicken burgers & tomato salsa

Calories per serving **299**
Serves **4**
Preparation time **15 minutes**,
    plus chilling
Cooking time **6–8 minutes**

1 **garlic clove**, crushed
3 **spring onions**, finely sliced
1 tablespoon **pesto**
2 tablespoons chopped **mixed
    herbs**, such as parsley,
    tarragon and thyme
375 g (12 oz) **minced
    chicken**
2 **sun-dried tomatoes**,
    finely chopped
1 teaspoon **olive oil**

Tomato salsa
250 g (8 oz) **cherry tomatoes**,
    quartered
1 **red chilli**, deseeded and
    finely chopped
1 tablespoon chopped
    coriander
grated rind and juice of 1 **lime**

To serve
toasted **wholemeal burger bun**
mixed salad leaves

Mix together all the burger ingredients, except the oil, in
a bowl. Divide the mixture into 4 and form into burgers.
Cover and chill for 30 minutes.

Meanwhile, combine all the salsa ingredients in a bowl.

Brush the burgers with oil and cook under a preheated
hot grill or on a barbecue for about 3–4 minutes on
each side until cooked through.

Serve each burger in a toasted burger bun with the
tomato salsa and salad leaves.

For turkey burgers with mint & yogurt sauce, make
the burgers as above, replacing the minced chicken with
375 g (12 oz) lean minced turkey. Instead of the salsa,
make a sauce by combining 5 tablespoons low-fat
natural yogurt, 1 deseeded and finely chopped red chilli,
1 tablespoon roughly chopped mint and a large pinch of
ground cumin in a bowl. Cook and serve the burgers as
above with the mint and yogurt sauce.

ginger scallops with asparagus

Calories per serving **248**
Serves **4**
Preparation time **10 minutes**,
    plus marinating
Cooking time **8–10 minutes**

12 **scallops**
2 **spring onions**, thinly sliced
finely grated rind of **1 lime**
1 tablespoon **ginger cordial**
2 tablespoons **extra-virgin
    olive oil**, plus extra for
    drizzling
250 g (8 oz) thin **asparagus
    spears**
juice of ½ **lime**
mixed salad leaves
salt and **pepper**
chervil sprigs, to garnish

Cut each scallop in half and place the pieces in a non-metallic bowl.

Mix together the spring onions, lime rind, ginger cordial and half the oil in a separate bowl. Season to taste and pour this dressing over the scallops. Leave to marinate for 15 minutes.

Meanwhile, put the asparagus in a steamer, cover and cook for 5–8 minutes until tender. Toss with the remaining oil and the lime juice. Season to taste and keep warm.

Heat a large nonstick frying pan until hot, add the scallops and fry for 1 minute on each side until golden and just cooked through. Add the marinade juices and heat through.

Arrange the asparagus spears, salad leaves and chervil sprigs on 4 serving plates with the scallops and any pan juices, then serve.

For scallops with Parma ham, wash and cut the scallops, then marinate in 2 crushed garlic cloves, the lime rind and all the oil, omitting the spring onions and ginger cordial. Meanwhile, remove the fat from 4 slices of Parma ham, then cook under a preheated hot grill for 2–3 minutes until golden and crisp. Leave to cool, then break the ham into large pieces. Cook the scallops as above and serve with the ham and remaining ingredients. Omit the asparagus.

crab & coriander cakes

Calories per serving **185**
Serves **6**
Preparation time **20 minutes**
Cooking time **10 minutes**

375 g (12 oz) **canned crabmeat**, drained
250 g (8 oz) **cold mashed potatoes**
2 tablespoons chopped **coriander**
bunch of **spring onions**, finely sliced
grated rind and juice of ½ **lemon**
2 **eggs**, beaten
flour, for coating
150 g (5 oz) **fresh white breadcrumbs**
1 tablespoon **vegetable oil**
lime wedges, to serve

Mix together, in a large bowl, the crabmeat, mashed potatoes, coriander, spring onions, lemon rind and juice and half the beaten egg to bind.

Form the mixture into 12 cakes about 1 cm (½ inch) thick. Coat the cakes with flour, then dip into the remaining egg and then the breadcrumbs.

Heat the oil in a nonstick frying pan and fry the cakes for about 10 minutes until golden, turning once or twice.

Drain the cakes on kitchen paper, then serve 2 cakes per person with a sweet red chilli sauce or tomato salsa, if liked (remembering to count the extra calories), and with lime wedges.

For cod & dill cakes, prepare the cakes as above, using 375 g (12 oz) cooked cod fillet, skinned and flaked, in place of the crabmeat and 2 tablespoons chopped dill instead of the coriander. Add 2 tablespoons drained and chopped capers to the mix before shaping, coating and frying as above. Serve with a little half-fat soured cream.

parsley & garlic sardines

Calories per serving **180**
Serves **6**
Preparation time **10 minutes**,
  plus chilling (optional)
Cooking time **5 minutes**

12 **fresh sardines**, cleaned,
  or use fillets if preferred

Marinade
50 g (2 oz) chopped **parsley**
1 teaspoon **freshly ground
  black pepper**
1 **garlic clove**, crushed
finely grated rind and juice
  of 1 **lemon**
2 tablespoons **white wine**
1 tablespoon **olive oil**

Put all the marinade ingredients in a small saucepan. Bring to the boil, then remove from the heat.

Place the sardines on a prepared barbecue or on a preheated hot griddle or under a hot grill. Cook for 1–2 minutes on each side until crisp and golden.

Arrange the sardines in a single layer in a shallow serving dish. Pour the dressing over the sardines and serve hot. Alternatively, cover and chill for at least 1 hour before serving cold.

For harissa & almond sardines, combine the ingredients for the marinade in a bowl, replacing the white wine with 1½ teaspoons harissa paste. Cook the sardines as above, arrange in a shallow dish, then spoon over the prepared marinade. Cover and chill for at least 1 hour, occasionally turning the sardines in the marinade. Scatter with 1 tablespoon toasted flaked almonds and serve as above.

lettuce wrappers with crab

Calories per serving **50**
Serves **4**
Preparation time **30 minutes**

1 **fresh cooked crab**, about
    500 g (1 lb), cleaned
4 small **iceberg lettuce
    leaves**
salt and **pepper**

Cucumber relish
¼ **cucumber**, finely diced
3 **spring onions**, thinly sliced
½ large **red chilli**, deseeded
    and finely chopped
2 tablespoons **white wine
    vinegar**
1 teaspoon **light soy sauce**
1 teaspoon **caster sugar**
4 teaspoons finely chopped
    mint or **coriander**

Make the relish by mixing all the ingredients in a bowl with a little salt and pepper.

Twist and remove the 2 large claws and spider-like legs from the crab and set aside. With the crab upside down, pull away the ball-like, spongy lungs. Check that the small sac and any green matter have been removed, then scoop the brown meat and skin from under the shell on to a plate. Break up the crabmeat with a spoon.

Put the crab claws into a plastic bag and hit once or twice with a rolling pin to break the shells. Then, working on one claw at a time, peel away the shell, removing the white flesh with a small knife and a skewer. Add to the brown crabmeat.

When ready to serve, spoon the crab into the lettuce leaves and top with spoonfuls of the cucumber relish. Roll up and eat with your fingers.

For lettuce wrappers with spicy prawns, make the relish as above. Toss 350 g (11½ oz) raw peeled king prawns in ½ tablespoon Thai red curry paste in a bowl until well coated. Cover and chill for 30 minutes. Heat 2 teaspoons groundnut oil in a nonstick frying pan, add the prawns and stir-fry for 3–4 minutes until they turn pink and are cooked through. Toss the prawns into the relish and serve spooned into the lettuce leaves.

tiger prawns with pancetta

Calories per serving **187**
Serves **4**
Preparation time **5 minutes**
Cooking time **7–8 minutes**

1 teaspoon **olive oil**
15 g (½ oz) **unsalted butter**
50 g (2 oz) **pancetta** or
    smoked bacon, excess fat
    removed, finely chopped
500 g (1 lb) **raw tiger prawns,
    peeled but tails left intact**
grated rind and juice of
    1 **lemon**
large bunch of **watercress**

Heat the oil and butter in a frying pan, add the pancetta
or smoked bacon and fry for 3–4 minutes until crisp.

Add the prawns and fry for 1 minute on each side
or until they turn pink. Sprinkle over the lemon rind
and juice and fry for a further 1 minute, then add the
watercress and combine well. Divide between 4 plates
and serve immediately.

For tiger prawns & chorizo with rocket, omit the
olive oil, butter and pancetta. Finely slice 50 g (2 oz)
chorizo and dry-fry in a large nonstick frying pan over
a low heat until crispy and some of its juices have been
released. Increase the heat to high, toss in the prawns
and continue as above, replacing the watercress with
100 g (3½ oz) wild rocket.

chilli & coriander fish parcel

Calories per serving **127**
Serves **1**
Preparation time **15 minutes**,
  plus marinating and chilling
Cooking time **15 minutes**

125 g (4 oz) **cod**, **coley** or
  haddock fillet
2 teaspoons **fresh lemon juice**
1 tablespoon **coriander leaves**
1 **garlic clove**
1 **green chilli**, deseeded
  and chopped
¼ teaspoon **sugar**
2 teaspoons **low-fat natural
  yogurt**

To garnish
coriander sprigs
sliced **green chillies**

Place the fish in a non-metallic dish and sprinkle with
the lemon juice. Cover and leave to marinate in the
refrigerator for 15–20 minutes.

Put the coriander, garlic and chilli in a food processor
or blender and process until the mixture forms a paste.
Add the sugar and yogurt and briefly process to blend.

Lay the fish on a sheet of foil. Coat the fish on both
sides with the paste. Gather up the foil loosely and turn
over at the top to seal. Chill for at least 1 hour.

Place the parcel on a baking sheet and bake in a
preheated oven, 200°C (400°F), Gas Mark 6, for about
15 minutes until the fish is just cooked through.

Garnish with coriander sprigs and sliced green chillies
and serve immediately.

For spring onion & ginger fish parcel, place the
fish fillet on a sheet of foil. Omit the above marinade.
Combine 1 teaspoon peeled and chopped fresh root
ginger and 2 thinly sliced spring onions with a pinch of
caster sugar and the juice and grated rind of ½ lime.
Rub the mixture all over the fish, then seal and marinate
the parcel as above for 30 minutes. Bake as above.

crab & noodle asian wraps

Calories per serving **199**
Serves **4**
Preparation time **15 minutes**,
    plus standing
Cooking time **5 minutes**

200 g (7 oz) **rice noodles**
1 bunch of **spring onions**,
    finely sliced
1.5 cm (¾ inch) piece of
    fresh root ginger, peeled
    and grated
1 **garlic clove**, finely sliced
1 **red chilli**, finely chopped
2 tablespoons chopped
    coriander
1 tablespoon chopped **mint**
¼ **cucumber**, cut into fine
    matchsticks
2 x 175 g (6 oz) cans
    crabmeat, drained, or
    300 g (10 oz) **fresh white
    crabmeat**
1 tablespoon **sesame oil**
1 tablespoon **sweet chilli
    sauce**
1 teaspoon **Thai fish sauce**
16 **Chinese pancakes** or
    **Vietnamese ricepaper
    wrappers**

Cook the noodles according to the packet instructions.
Drain, then refresh under cold running water.

Mix together all the other ingredients, except the
pancakes or ricepaper wrappers, in a large bowl. Add
the noodles and toss to mix. Cover and leave to stand
for 10 minutes to allow the flavours to develop, then
transfer to a serving dish.

To serve, top the pancakes or ricepapers with some of
the crab and noodle mixture and roll up to eat, allowing
4 wraps per person.

For prawn & peanut wraps, make the mixture as
above, replacing the crab with 200 g (7 oz) small
cooked peeled prawns and adding 20 g (¾ oz) chopped
peanuts. Stir in the juice of 1 lime and wrap as above.

red pepper & feta rolls with olives

Calories per serving **146**
Serves **4**
Preparation time **15 minutes**,
 plus cooling
Cooking time **7–8 minutes**

2 **red peppers**, cored,
 deseeded and quartered
 lengthways
100 g (3½ oz) **feta cheese**,
 thinly sliced or crumbled
16 **basil leaves**
16 **black olives**, pitted
 and halved
15 g (½ oz) **pine nuts**, toasted
1 tablespoon **pesto**
1 tablespoon **fat-free
 French dressing**

Place the peppers skin-side up on a baking sheet
under a preheated hot grill and cook for 7–8 minutes
until the skins are blackened. Remove the peppers and
place them in a plastic bag. Fold over the top to seal and
leave to cool for 20 minutes, then remove the skins.

Lay the skinned pepper quarters on a board and layer
up the feta, basil, olives and pine nuts on each one.

Carefully roll up the peppers and secure each one
with a cocktail stick. Place 2 pepper rolls on each of
4 serving plates.

Whisk together the pesto and French dressing in a small
bowl and drizzle over the pepper rolls. Serve with rocket,
if liked (remembering to count the extra calories).

For red pepper, ricotta & sun-dried tomato rolls,

grill and skin the peppers as above. Mix 5 chopped
sun-dried tomatoes into 100 g (3½ oz) ricotta cheese,
also stirring in the basil and pine nuts. Omit the feta and
black olives. Season with salt and pepper and use to top
the pepper quarters. Roll up and serve as above.

caponata ratatouille

Calories per serving **90**
Serves **6**
Preparation time **20 minutes**
Cooking time **40 minutes**

1 tablespoon **olive oil**
750 g (1½ lb) **aubergines**, cut
    into 1 cm (½ inch) chunks
1 large **onion**, cut into 1 cm
    (½ inch) chunks
3 **celery sticks**, roughly
    chopped
a little **wine** (optional)
2 large **beef tomatoes**,
    skinned (see page 162)
    and deseeded
1 teaspoon chopped **thyme**
¼–½ teaspoon **cayenne**
    pepper
2 tablespoons **capers**, drained
handful of **pitted green olives**
4 tablespoons **white wine**
    vinegar
1 tablespoon **sugar**
1–2 tablespoons **cocoa**
    powder (optional)
pepper

To garnish
toasted, chopped **almonds**
chopped **parsley**

Heat the oil in a nonstick frying pan until very hot, add the aubergine and fry for about 15 minutes until very soft. Add a little boiling water to prevent sticking if necessary.

Meanwhile, place the onion and celery in a saucepan with a little water or wine. Cook for 5 minutes until tender but still firm.

Add the tomatoes, thyme, cayenne pepper and aubergine and onions. Cook for 15 minutes, stirring occasionally. Add the capers, olives, wine vinegar, sugar and cocoa powder, if using, and cook for 2–3 minutes.

Season with pepper and scatter with almonds and parsley. Divide between 6 bowls and serve immediately.

For red pepper & courgette caponata, grill and skin 2 red and 2 yellow peppers (see page 80). Cook the onion and celery as above, then continue as above, adding the skinned peppers and 500 g (1 lb) thickly sliced courgettes instead of the aubergines, and omitting the thyme and cocoa powder.

courgette & mint frittatas

Calories per serving **200**
Serves **6**
Preparation time **10 minutes**
Cooking time **about 30
    minutes**

1 tablespoon **olive oil**
1 **onion**, finely chopped
2 **courgettes**, about 375
    g (12 oz) in total, halved
    lengthways and thinly sliced
6 **eggs**
300 ml (½ pint) **skimmed milk**
3 tablespoons grated
    Parmesan cheese
2 tablespoons chopped **mint**,
    plus extra leaves to garnish
    (optional)
salt and **pepper**

Tomato sauce
1 tablespoon **olive oil**
1 **onion**, finely chopped
1–2 **garlic cloves**, crushed
    (optional)
500 g (1 lb) **plum tomatoes**,
    chopped

Lightly oil a 12-hole muffin tin.

Make the sauce. Heat the oil in a saucepan, add
the onion and fry for 5 minutes, stirring occasionally,
until softened and just beginning to brown. Add the
garlic, if using, and the tomatoes and season with salt
and pepper. Stir and simmer for 5 minutes until the
tomatoes are soft. Purée in a blender or food processor
until smooth, then pass through a sieve into a bowl
and keep warm.

Heat the oil in a frying pan, add the onion and fry
until softened and just beginning to brown. Add the
courgettes, stir to combine and cook for 3–4 minutes
until softened but not browned.

Beat together the eggs, milk, Parmesan and mint in a
bowl, then stir in the courgettes. Season well and divide
the mixture between the 12 sections of the prepared
tin. Bake in a preheated oven, 190°C (375°F), Gas Mark
5, for about 15 minutes until lightly browned, well risen
and the egg mixture has set.

Leave the frittatas in the tin for 1–2 minutes, then
loosen the edges with a knife. Turn out and arrange on
6 plates with the warm tomato sauce. Garnish with extra
mint leaves, if liked.

For garlicky rocket frittatas, make the tomato sauce
to serve as above. For the frittatas, omit the courgettes.
Soften the onions as above, then add 2 crushed garlic
cloves, stir for 1 minute and remove from the heat.
Beat together the eggs, milk and Parmesan as above,
replacing the mint with 75 g (3 oz) roughly chopped
rocket. Tip in the cooked onions and bake as above.

goats' cheese & herb soufflés

Calories per soufflé **277**
Serves **4**
Preparation time **10 minutes**
Cooking time **13–15 minutes**

25 g (1 oz) **polyunsaturated margarine**
50 g (2 oz) **plain flour**
300 ml (½ pint) **skimmed milk**
4 **eggs**, separated
100 g (3½ oz) **goats' cheese**, crumbled
1 tablespoon chopped **mixed herbs**, such as parsley, chives and thyme
1 tablespoon grated **Parmesan cheese**
75 g (3 oz) **rocket leaves**
2 tablespoons **fat-free salad dressing**
salt and **pepper**

Melt the margarine in a medium saucepan, add the flour and cook, stirring, for 1 minute. Gradually add the milk, whisking all the time, and cook for 2 minutes until the roux has thickened.

Remove the pan from the heat. Beat in the egg yolks one at a time, then stir in the goats' cheese. Season well with salt and pepper.

Whisk the egg whites in a large bowl until they form firm peaks, then gradually fold them into the cheese mixture with the herbs. Transfer to 4 lightly oiled ramekins, sprinkle over the Parmesan, then bake in a preheated oven, 190°C (375°F), Gas Mark 5, for 10–12 minutes until risen and golden.

Toss together the rocket and dressing in a bowl and serve with the soufflés.

For Gruyère & mustard soufflé, cook the flour in the margarine as above, stirring in 2 teaspoons English mustard powder. Continue as above, replacing the goats' cheese with 75 g (3 oz) grated Gruyère and omitting the Parmesan.

chilli & melon sorbet with ham

Calories per serving **125**
Serves **6**
Preparation time **35 minutes**,
  plus freezing

1½ **cantaloupe melons**,
  quartered and deseeded
12 slices of **Serrano ham**,
  Prosciutto crudo or **Parma**
  ham, fat removed

Sorbet
1 **cantaloupe melon**, halved,
  peeled and deseeded
2 tablespoons chopped **mint**
½–1 large **red chilli**,
  deseeded and finely
  chopped (to taste), plus
  strips of chilli to garnish
1 **egg white**

Make the sorbet. Scoop the melon flesh into a food processor or blender and blend until smooth. Stir in the mint and add chilli to taste.

Transfer the mixture to an ice cream maker and churn until thick. Alternatively, pour the mixture into a plastic box and freeze for 4 hours, beating once or twice to break up the ice crystals.

Mix in the egg white and continue churning until the sorbet is thick enough to scoop. If you are not serving it immediately, transfer the sorbet to a plastic box and store in the freezer. Otherwise, freeze for a minimum of 2 hours until firm.

Arrange the melon quarters and ham on 6 serving plates. Use warm spoons to scoop out the sorbet and put 2 spoonfuls of sorbet on top of each melon quarter. Garnish with strips of chilli and serve immediately.

For honeyed peaches, to serve with the ham instead of the sorbet and melon quarters, make a dressing using 1 tablespoon extra-virgin olive oil, 2 tablespoons chopped mint, ½ deseeded and finely chopped red chilli and 1 teaspoon clear honey. Cut 5 peaches into wedges and stir into the dressing. Leave to marinate for 30 minutes, then serve with the ham slices.

red pepper rouille & vegetables

Calories per serving **154**
Serves **6**
Preparation time **30 minutes**,
  plus marinating and cooling
Cooking time **30–35 minutes**

4 tablespoons **olive oil**
2–3 **garlic cloves**, finely
  chopped
3 large pinches of **saffron
  threads**
3 mixed **red** and **orange
  peppers**, cored, deseeded
  and each cut into 6 strips
3 **courgettes**, about 100 g
  (3½ oz) each
2 **onions**, cut into wedges
salt and **pepper**

Rouille

4 **plum tomatoes** or 250 g
  (8 oz) in total
1 **red pepper**, cored,
  deseeded and quartered
1 **garlic clove**, finely chopped
large pinch of **ground
  pimentón** (smoked paprika)
1 tablespoon **olive oil**

Put the oil for the vegetables in a large plastic bag
with the garlic, saffron and salt and pepper. Add the
vegetables, grip the top edge of the bag to seal and
toss together. Leave to marinate for at least 30 minutes.

Make the rouille. Put the tomatoes and red pepper into
a roasting tin. Sprinkle with the garlic, pimentón and salt
and pepper, then drizzle over the oil. Roast in a preheated
oven, 220°C (425°F), Gas Mark 7, for 15 minutes.

Leave to cool, then peel the skins from the tomatoes and
pepper. Purée the flesh in a blender or food processor
with any juices from the roasting tin until smooth. Spoon
into a serving bowl and set aside.

Tip the saffron vegetables into a large roasting tin and
cook in a preheated oven, 220°C (425°F), Gas Mark 7,
for 15–20 minutes, turning once until browned. Spoon
the vegetables into 6 bowls and serve with spoonfuls
of the rouille, reheated if necessary.

For potato puffs, to serve with the rouille instead of
the saffron vegetables, cut 1 kg (2 lb) new potatoes
in half and lay them, cut-side up, in a single layer in an
ovenproof dish. Scatter with sea salt and black pepper
and roast (without any oil) in a preheated oven, 220°C
(425°F), Gas Mark 7, for 30–35 minutes until cooked
through and puffed up. Serve with the rouille.

vietnamese-style noodle salad

Calories per serving **271**
Serves **4**
Preparation time **20 minutes**
Cooking time **4 minutes**

200 g (7 oz) **fine rice noodles**
½ **cucumber**, deseeded and
cut into matchsticks
1 **carrot**, cut into matchsticks
150 g (5 oz) **bean sprouts**
125 g (4 oz) **mangetout**,
cut into thin strips
2 tablespoons chopped
coriander
2 tablespoons chopped **mint**
1 **red chilli**, deseeded and
finely sliced
2 tablespoons chopped
unsalted peanuts,
to garnish

Dressing
1 tablespoon **sunflower** or
groundnut oil
½ teaspoon **caster sugar**
1 tablespoon **Thai fish sauce**
2 tablespoons **lime juice**

Bring a large saucepan of water to the boil, then turn off the heat and add the rice noodles. Cover and leave to cook for 4 minutes, or according to the packet instructions, until just tender. Drain the noodles and cool immediately in a bowl of ice-cold water.

Meanwhile, make the dressing by placing the ingredients in a screw-top jar, adding the lid and shaking until the sugar has dissolved.

Drain the noodles and return to the bowl. Pour over half of the dressing, then tip in the vegetables, herbs and chilli. Toss until well combined.

Heap the noodle salad on 4 serving plates and drizzle with the remaining dressing. Serve scattered with the chopped peanuts.

green bean & asparagus salad

Calories per serving **285**
Serves **6**
Preparation time **10 minutes**
Cooking time **8 minutes**

250 g (8 oz) **fine green
    beans**, trimmed
400 g (13 oz) **asparagus**,
    trimmed
6 **eggs**
100 g (3½ oz) **rocket leaves**
75 g (3 oz) **pitted black olives**
75 g (3 oz) **Parmesan
    cheese**, cut into shavings
salt and **pepper**

Dressing

5 tablespoons **olive oil**
3 teaspoons **black olive pesto**
    or **tapenade**
3 teaspoons **balsamic vinegar**

Put the green beans in the top of a steamer, cover and cook for 3 minutes. Add the asparagus and cook for a further 5 minutes until the vegetables are just tender.

Meanwhile, put the eggs into a small saucepan, cover with cold water and bring to the boil. Simmer for 6 minutes until still soft in the centre.

Make the dressing by mixing together the oil, pesto and vinegar in a small bowl with a little salt and pepper.

Arrange the rocket in the centre of 6 serving plates. Drain and rinse the eggs with cold water. Drain again, gently peel away the shells and halve each egg. Place 2 halves on each mound of rocket. Arrange the beans and asparagus around the edge, then drizzle with the dressing. Add the olives and top with the Parmesan shavings. Serve immediately.

For Tenderstem broccoli & olive salad, omit the beans and asparagus and steam 500 g (1 lb) Tenderstem broccoli as above for 5 minutes. Cook the eggs as above, shell and quarter. Arrange the rocket on 6 plates, then scatter with the eggs and broccoli. Continue with the dressing, olives and Parmesan as above.

potato & onion tortilla

Calories per serving **296**
Serves **6**
Preparation time **10 minutes**
Cooking time **30 minutes**

750 g (1 ½ lb) **baking
  potatoes**, peeled and
  sliced very thinly
4 tablespoons **olive oil**
2 large **onions**, thinly sliced
6 **eggs**, beaten
salt and **pepper**

Toss the potatoes in a bowl with a little seasoning.
Heat the oil in a medium-sized, heavy-based frying pan,
add the potatoes and fry very gently for 10 minutes,
turning frequently, until softened but not browned.

Add the onions and fry gently for a further 5 minutes
without browning. Spread the potatoes and onions in
an even layer in the pan then reduce the heat as low
as possible.

Pour over the eggs, cover and cook very gently for
about 15 minutes until the eggs have set. (If the
centre of the omelette is too wet, put the pan under
a preheated medium grill to finish cooking.) Tip the
tortilla on to a plate, cut into 6 wedges and serve warm
or cold with a rocket, herb and tomato salad, if liked
(remembering to count the extra calories).

For pepper & artichoke tortilla, drain 100 g (3½ oz)
marinated artichokes in olive oil, reserving the oil. Heat
1 tablespoon of the oil in a frying pan and cook 2 red
and 1 yellow cored, deseeded and sliced peppers for
5–6 minutes until starting to soften. Roughly chop the
artichokes and add to the pan with 1 small chopped
onion, and 1 tablespoon chopped mint. Spread into an
even layer and reduce the heat as low as possible, then
pour over the eggs and cook as above.

mushroom crêpes

Calories per serving **112**
Serves **4**
Preparation time **20 minutes**
Cooking time **30 minutes**

50 g (2 oz) **plain flour**
150 ml (¼ pint) **skimmed milk**
1 small **egg**, beaten
1 teaspoon **olive oil**
salt and **pepper**
flat leaf parsley sprigs,
   to garnish

Filling
300 g (10 oz) **chestnut mushrooms**, chopped
bunch of **spring onions**,
   finely chopped
1 **garlic clove**, chopped
400 g (13 oz) can **chopped tomatoes**, drained
2 tablespoons chopped
   oregano

Put the flour, milk, egg and salt and pepper in a blender or food processor and blend until smooth, or whisk with a fork in a bowl.

Heat a few drops of the oil in a nonstick frying pan. Pour in a ladleful of the batter and cook for 1 minute. Carefully flip the pancake over and cook the other side. Slide the pancake out of the pan on to greaseproof paper. Make 3 more pancakes in the same way, adding a few more drops of oil to the pan between each one, and stack the pancakes between sheets of greaseproof paper.

Meanwhile, make the filling. Put all the ingredients in a saucepan and cook for 5 minutes, stirring occasionally.

Divide the filling between the pancakes, reserving a little of the mixture to serve, then roll them up.

Transfer to an ovenproof dish and bake in a preheated oven, 180°C (350°F), Gas Mark 4, for 20 minutes. Serve with the reheated reserved mushroom mixture, garnished with parsley sprigs.

For ratatouille-filled crêpes, put 2 chopped courgettes, 1 cored, deseeded and chopped red pepper, 1 chopped red onion, a 400 g (13 oz) can chopped tomatoes and a few basil leaves in a large saucepan and simmer for 6–8 minutes, stirring occasionally. Make the pancakes as above, then fill with the courgette mixture and bake as above.

leek & tomato filo tarts

Calories per serving **135**
Serves **4**
Preparation time **20 minutes,**
  plus soaking
Cooking time **30 minutes**

8 **sun-dried tomatoes**
2 **leeks**, trimmed and
  thinly sliced
300 ml (½ pint) **white wine**
2 tablespoons **skimmed milk**
1 small **egg**, separated
50 g (2 oz) **low-fat soft
  cheese**
12 pieces of **filo pastry**,
  each about 15 cm
  (6 inches) square
salt and **pepper**

Put the sun-dried tomatoes in a small heatproof bowl and pour over enough boiling water to cover. Leave to soak for 20 minutes.

Meanwhile, put the leeks and wine in a saucepan and bring to the boil, then reduce the heat and simmer until the liquid has evaporated. Remove the pan from the heat and stir in the milk, egg yolk and cheese. Season with salt and pepper.

Beat the egg white lightly in a jug. Brush a filo pastry square with a little of the egg white and use it to line the base and sides of a 10 cm (4 inch) tart tin. Brush 2 more filo squares and lay these on top, each at a slight angle to the first, allowing the edges to overlap the rim. Repeat with the remaining squares to line 3 more tart tins.

Place a spoonful of the cooked leek mixture in each pastry case. Lay 2 of the drained, rehydrated tomatoes on top of each tart and cover with the remaining leek mixture. Season again and bake in a preheated oven, 200°C (400°F), Gas Mark 6, for 20 minutes, covering the tarts with pieces of foil after 10 minutes. Serve hot, with cherry tomatoes and sliced red onion if liked (remembering to count the extra calories).

red pepper & spring onion dip

Calories per serving
  (dip only) **60**
Serves **4**
Preparation time **10 minutes**
Cooking time **30–40 minutes**

1 large **red pepper**, cored,
  deseeded and quartered
2 **garlic cloves**, unpeeled
250 ml (8 fl oz) **low-fat
  natural yogurt**
2 **spring onions**, finely
  chopped, plus extra
  to garnish
pepper
selection of **raw vegetables**,
  such as carrots, cucumber,
  peppers, fennel, tomatoes,
  baby corn, mangetout, celery
  and courgettes, cut into
  batons, to serve

Slightly flatten the pepper quarters and place on a baking sheet. Wrap the garlic in foil and place on the sheet. Roast in a preheated oven, 220°C (425°F), Gas Mark 7, for 30–40 minutes until the pepper is slightly charred and the garlic is soft.

When cool enough to handle, remove the skin from the pepper and discard. Transfer the flesh to a bowl.

Squeeze the roasted garlic flesh from the cloves into the bowl.

Using a fork, roughly mash the pepper and garlic together. Stir in the yogurt and spring onions.

Garnish with extra chopped spring onion, season to taste with pepper and serve with the vegetable batons.

For aubergine & yogurt dip, roast a whole aubergine in a preheated oven, 220°C (425°F), Gas Mark 7, with the garlic for 30–40 minutes, omitting the red pepper. If the aubergine is still not tender after the cooking time, carefully turn it over and bake for a further 10–15 minutes until very soft. Cut the aubergine in half and scoop the flesh out on to a chopping board. Roughly chop with a handful of basil leaves and season with salt and pepper. Stir into the yogurt and spring onions, and add the roasted garlic. Serve with the vegetable batons.

main meals

butternut squash & ricotta frittata

Calories per serving **248**
Serves **6**
Preparation time **10 minutes**
Cooking time **25–30 minutes**

1 tablespoon **extra-virgin**
   rapeseed oil
1 **red onion**, thinly sliced
450 g (14½ oz) peeled
   and deseeded **butternut**
   squash, diced
8 **eggs**
2 tablespoons chopped **sage**
1 tablespoon chopped **thyme**
125 g (4 oz) **ricotta cheese**
salt and **pepper**

Heat the oil in a large, deep frying pan with an ovenproof handle over a medium-low heat, add the onion and butternut squash, then cover loosely and cook gently, stirring frequently, for 18–20 minutes until softened and golden.

Beat together the eggs, herbs and ricotta lightly in a jug, then season well with salt and pepper and pour over the squash mixture.

Cook for 2–3 minutes until the egg is almost set, stirring occasionally to prevent the base from burning.

Slide the pan under a preheated grill, keeping the handle away from the heat, and cook for 3–4 minutes until the egg is set and the frittata is golden. Slice into 6 wedges and serve hot.

For poached egg-topped butternut salad, toss the diced butternut squash and thickly sliced red onion in the rapeseed oil in a roasting tin and roast in a preheated oven, 200°C (400°F), Gas Mark 6, for 20 minutes. Remove from the oven and leave to cool while you poach the eggs. Bring a saucepan of water to the boil, swirl the water with a spoon and crack in an egg, allowing the white to wrap around the yolk. Simmer for 3 minutes, then remove and keep warm. Repeat with 5 more eggs. Toss the warm roasted squash and onion with 125 g (4 oz) baby spinach leaves and divide between 6 serving plates. Top each salad with a poached egg, then spoon a little ricotta cheese over each, sprinkle with the herbs and serve.

lamb cutlets with herbed crust

Calories per serving **280**
Serves **4**
Preparation time **10 minutes**
Cooking time **12–14 minutes**

12 **lean lamb cutlets**, about
40 g (1½ oz) each
2 tablespoons **pesto**
3 tablespoons **granary**
breadcrumbs
1 tablespoon chopped
walnuts, toasted
1 teaspoon **vegetable oil**
2 **garlic cloves**, crushed
625 g (1¼ lb) **greens**, finely
shredded and blanched

Heat a nonstick frying pan or griddle until hot, add
the cutlets and cook for 1 minute on each side, then
transfer to a baking sheet.

Mix together the pesto, breadcrumbs and walnuts in a
bowl, then use to top one side of the cutlets, pressing
down lightly. Place in a preheated oven, 200°C (400°F),
Gas Mark 6, for 10–12 minutes.

Meanwhile, heat the oil in a frying pan or wok, add
the garlic and stir-fry for 1 minute, then add the greens
and stir-fry for a further 3–4 minutes until tender.

Serve the lamb and greens with some baby carrots,
if liked (remembering to count the extra calories).

For lamb cutlets with herbed caper dressing, make
a dressing by combining 1 tablespoon each of chopped
flat leaf parsley, mint and basil in a small bowl. Stir in
1 crushed garlic clove, 1 tablespoon drained and chopped
capers and 2 tablespoons extra-virgin olive oil. Griddle
the cutlets for 2–3 minutes on each side, depending on
whether you like your lamb medium or well done, omit
the breadcrumb topping, and serve with the vegetables
as above and a generous drizzle of the dressing.

beef skewers with dipping sauce

Calories per serving **140**
Serves **4**
Preparation time **10 minutes**,
   plus marinating
Cooking time **2–3 minutes**

1 tablespoon **sweet chilli
   sauce**
½ teaspoon **cumin seeds**,
   toasted
½ teaspoon **ground coriander**
1 teaspoon **olive oil**
350 g (11½ oz) **lean rump
   steak**, cut into strips

Dipping sauce
1 tablespoon **sweet chilli
   sauce**
1 teaspoon **Thai fish sauce**
1 teaspoon **white wine
   vinegar**

To serve
2 tablespoons chopped
   coriander
1 tablespoon **unsalted
   peanuts**, roughly chopped

Mix together the sweet chilli sauce, cumin seeds,
ground coriander and oil in a non-metallic bowl. Add
the meat and stir well to coat, then cover and leave
to marinate in a cool place for 30 minutes.

Thread the meat on to 4 bamboo skewers that have
been soaked in water for at least 20 minutes. Cook
on a hot griddle or under a preheated hot grill for
2–3 minutes until cooked through.

Meanwhile, mix together the sauce ingredients in a
small serving bowl. Serve the skewers with the sauce,
scattered with the coriander and peanuts.

For Thai-style salad, to serve with the skewers,
combine 1 grated carrot, ¼ thinly sliced cucumber
and 10 quartered cherry tomatoes in a bowl. Make the
dipping sauce as above, adding 1 teaspoon groundnut
oil. Toss it into the salad ingredients with the coriander
and peanuts used as garnish above, and serve the
skewers with the salad and lime wedges.

chicken & spinach curry

Calories per serving **205**
Serves **4**
Preparation time **15 minutes**
Cooking time **25 minutes**

1 tablespoon **vegetable oil**
4 **skinless chicken breast
    fillets**, about 125 g (4 oz)
    each, halved lengthways
1 **onion**, sliced
2 **garlic cloves**, chopped
1 **green chilli**, chopped
4 **cardamom pods**, lightly
    crushed
1 teaspoon **cumin seeds**
1 teaspoon **dried chilli flakes**
1 teaspoon **ground ginger**
1 teaspoon **ground turmeric**
250 g (8 oz) **baby spinach
    leaves**
300 g (10 oz) **tomatoes**,
    chopped
150 ml (¼ pint) **low-fat
    Greek yogurt**
2 tablespoons chopped
    coriander, plus extra sprigs
    to garnish

Heat the oil in a large frying pan or wok, add the
chicken, onion, garlic and chilli and fry for 4–5 minutes
until the chicken begins to brown and the onion softens.
Add the cardamoms, cumin seeds, dried chilli flakes,
ginger and turmeric and fry for a further 1 minute.

Add the spinach, cover and cook gently until the spinach
wilts, then stir in the tomatoes, re-cover and simmer
for 15 minutes or until the chicken is cooked through,
removing the lid for the last 5 minutes of cooking.

Stir the yogurt and chopped coriander into the curry, then
scatter over coriander sprigs to garnish. Serve with boiled
rice, if liked (remembering to count the extra calories).

For curried chicken kebabs & spinach salad,

cut the chicken into strips and put in a non-metallic
bowl with 1 chopped onion and 4 quartered tomatoes,
then toss with the garlic, chilli and spices. Thread on to
8 metal skewers, then cook under a preheated grill for
4–5 minutes on each side or until the chicken is cooked
through. Meanwhile, make a raita by mixing together
150 ml (5 fl oz) low-fat natural yogurt, ½ cucumber,
grated, and 2 tablespoons chopped mint in a bowl.
Serve 2 kebabs per person on a bed of baby spinach
leaves with the raita.

thai-style monkfish kebabs

Calories per serving **192**
Serves **4**
Preparation time **15 minutes**,
  plus marinating
Cooking time **10 minutes**

500–750 g (1–1½ lb)
  monkfish tails, skinned
  and cut into large cubes
1 **onion,** quartered and
  layers separated
8 **mushrooms**
1 **courgette,** cut into 8 pieces
vegetable oil, for brushing
lime wedges, to serve

Marinade
grated rind and juice of 2 **limes**
1 **garlic clove,** finely chopped
2 tablespoons peeled and
  finely sliced **fresh root
  ginger**
2 **chillies,** red or green or
  1 of each, deseeded and
  finely chopped
2 **lemon grass stalks,**
  finely chopped
handful of chopped **coriander**
1 glass **red wine**
2 tablespoons **sesame oil**
pepper

Combine the ingredients for the marinade in a large non-metallic bowl. Add the fish to the marinade with the onion, mushrooms and courgette and mix until well coated. Cover and leave to marinate in the refrigerator for 1 hour.

Brush the rack of a grill pan lightly with oil to prevent the kebabs from sticking. Thread 4 metal skewers alternately with the chunks of fish, mushrooms, courgette and onion. Brush with a little oil and cook under a preheated hot grill for about 10 minutes, turning at intervals, until cooked through. Serve with lime wedges for squeezing over.

For Mediterranean monkfish kebabs, replace the above marinade with one using the grated rind and juice of 1 lemon, 2 chopped garlic cloves, 2 tablespoons olive oil and 1 tablespoon each of chopped thyme and rosemary. Use to marinate the monkfish and vegetables for 30 minutes, then thread on to 4 metal skewers and cook as above.

pumpkin & goats' cheese bake

Calories per serving **230**
Serves **4**
Preparation time **20 minutes**
Cooking time **25–30 minutes**

400 g (13 oz) **raw beetroot**,
    peeled and diced
625 g (1¼ lb) **pumpkin** or
    butternut squash, peeled,
    deseeded and cut into
    slightly larger dice than
    the beetroot
1 **red onion**, cut into wedges
2 tablespoons **olive oil**
2 teaspoons **fennel seeds**
2 small **goats' cheeses**,
    100 g (3½ oz) each
salt and **pepper**
chopped **rosemary**, to garnish

Put the vegetables into a roasting tin, drizzle with the oil and sprinkle with the fennel seeds and salt and pepper. Roast in a preheated oven, 200°C (400°F), Gas Mark 6, for 20–25 minutes, turning once, until well browned and tender.

Cut the goats' cheeses into thirds and nestle among the roasted vegetables. Sprinkle the cheeses with a little salt and pepper and drizzle with some of the pan juices.

Return the dish to the oven and cook for about 5 minutes until the cheese is just beginning to melt. Sprinkle with rosemary and serve immediately.

For penne with beetroot & pumpkin, roast the vegetables as above for 20–25 minutes, omitting the fennel seeds. Cook 175 g (6 oz) penne pasta in a saucepan of salted boiling water, then drain, reserving one ladleful of the cooking water. Return the pasta to the pan and add the roasted vegetables, a handful of torn basil leaves and the reserved cooking water. Omit the goats' cheese and rosemary. Place over a high heat, stirring, for 30 seconds and serve.

russian meatballs

Calories per serving **154**
Serves **4**
Preparation time **15 minutes**,
  plus chilling
Cooking time **about 1 hour**

375 g (12 oz) **5%-fat**
  minced beef
1 **onion**, roughly chopped
1 tablespoon **tomato purée**
1 teaspoon **dried mixed**
  herbs
salt and **pepper**
chopped **parsley** and **parsley**
  sprigs, to garnish

Tomato sauce
1 **red onion**, finely chopped
400 g (13 oz) can **chopped**
  tomatoes
pinch of **paprika**, plus extra
  to garnish
1 teaspoon **dried mixed**
  herbs

Put the minced beef, onion, tomato purée and dried mixed herbs in a food processor, season well with salt and pepper and blend until smooth. Shape the mixture into 12 balls, cover and chill for 30 minutes.

Meanwhile, put the tomato sauce ingredients in a saucepan and cook, uncovered, over a low heat for 15–20 minutes, stirring occasionally.

Season the sauce with salt and pepper and transfer to an ovenproof dish. Arrange the meatballs on top and place in a preheated oven, 180°C (350°F), Gas Mark 4, for 45 minutes. Sprinkle the meatballs with chopped parsley and paprika, garnish with parsley sprigs and serve with mashed potatoes, if liked (remembering to count the extra calories).

For spicy burgers with fresh tomato salsa, mix together the minced beef, finely diced onion, tomato purée and mixed dried herbs with 1 finely diced red chilli and 1 beaten egg in a bowl. Divide the mixture into 4 and shape each into a burger. Cover and chill for 30 minutes. Meanwhile, make a tomato salsa by mixing together 1 finely chopped red onion, 175 g (6 oz) diced cherry tomatoes, 2 tablespoons chopped coriander and a drizzle of balsamic vinegar in a bowl. Heat a griddle pan until hot, add the burgers and cook for 4–5 minutes on each side until cooked through. Serve topped with a spoonful of the tomato salsa.

herby baked chicken

Calories per serving **275**
Serves **4**
Preparation time **10 minutes**
Cooking time **35–45 minutes**

500 g (1 lb) **new potatoes**
4 **skinless chicken breast
fillets**, about 125 g (4 oz)
each
6 tablespoons **mixed herbs**,
such as parsley, chives,
chervil and mint
1 **garlic clove**, crushed
6 tablespoons **low-fat (less
than 3%) crème fraîche**
8 **baby leeks**
2 **chicory heads**, halved
lengthways
150 ml (¼ pint) **chicken stock**
pepper

Cook the potatoes in a saucepan of boiling water for 12–15 minutes until tender. Drain, then cut into bite-sized pieces.

Make a slit lengthways down the side of each chicken breast to form a pocket, ensuring that you do not cut all the way through. Mix together the herbs, garlic and crème fraîche, season well with pepper, then spoon a little into each chicken pocket.

Put the leeks, chicory and potatoes in an ovenproof dish. Pour over the stock, then lay the chicken breasts on top. Spoon over the remaining crème fraîche mixture, then bake in a preheated oven, 200°C (400°F), Gas Mark 6, for 25–30 minutes until the chicken is cooked through and the vegetables are tender.

For baked chicken with fennel & potatoes, cut the potatoes in half and place them in a large ovenproof dish with 1 large fennel bulb, trimmed and cut into quarters. Omit the leeks and chicory. Pour over the stock and bake in a preheated oven at 200°C (400°F), Gas Mark 6, for 20 minutes. Lay the chicken breasts over the vegetables. Combine 1 tablespoon chopped parsley with 1 tablespoon Dijon mustard and the crème fraîche, omitting the garlic, and spoon the mixture over the chicken. Return to the oven and bake for a further 25–30 minutes until cooked through.

pan-fried plaice & mustard sauce

Calories per serving **182**
Serves **4**
Preparation time **10 minutes**
Cooking time **10 minutes**

1 teaspoon **olive oil**
1 small **onion**, finely chopped
1 **garlic clove**, crushed
4 **plaice** or **sole fillets**, about
    150 g (5 oz) each
125 ml (4 fl oz) **dry white wine**
2 tablespoons **wholegrain**
    mustard
200 g (7 oz) **low-fat (less**
    than 3%) crème fraîche
2 tablespoons chopped
    mixed herbs

To serve
300 g (10 oz) steamed **baby**
    new potatoes
300 g (10 oz) steamed **green**
    beans

Heat the oil in a large frying pan, add the onion and garlic and fry for 3 minutes until softened.

Add the fish fillets and cook for 1 minute on each side, then add the wine and simmer to reduce by half.

Stir through the remaining ingredients and bring to the boil, then reduce the heat and simmer for 3–4 minutes until the sauce has thickened slightly and the fish is tender. Serve with steamed baby new potatoes and green beans.

For salmon with cucumber & crème fraîche, cook the onion and garlic as above. Omit the plaice or sole. Add 400 g (13 oz) skinned salmon, cut into chunks, and cook, stirring, for 1 minute. Add the wine, simmer as above, then add 1 tablespoon wholegrain mustard, the crème fraîche and ¼ cucumber, peeled and sliced. Cook for 2 minutes, then stir in 1 tablespoon chopped dill instead of the mixed herbs.

split pea & pepper patties

Calories per serving **312**
Serves **4**
Preparation **20 minutes**, plus
  cooling and chilling
Cooking time **45–50 minutes**

750 ml (1¼ pints) **Vegetable
  Stock** (see page 48)
3 **garlic cloves**, unpeeled
250 g (8 oz) **yellow split
  peas**, well rinsed
olive oil spray
2 **red peppers**, cored,
  deseeded and halved
1 **yellow pepper**, cored,
  deseeded and halved
1 **red onion**, quartered
1 tablespoon chopped **mint**,
  plus extra leaves to garnish
2 tablespoons **capers**, drained
  and chopped
plain flour, for dusting
salt and **pepper**

Tzatziki
½ **cucumber**, finely chopped
1 **garlic clove**, crushed
2 tablespoons chopped **mint**
300 ml (½ pint) **low-fat
  natural yogurt**

Bring the stock to the boil in a large saucepan. Peel and halve 1 of the garlic cloves, then add to the pan with the split peas and cook for 40 minutes until the split peas are tender. Drain, if necessary, then season with salt and pepper and leave to cool slightly.

Meanwhile, lightly spray a roasting tin with oil. Put the remaining garlic cloves in the tin with the peppers and onion and roast in a preheated oven, 200°C (400°F), Gas Mark 6, for 20 minutes. When cool enough to handle, squeeze the roasted garlic cloves from their skins and chop with the roasted vegetables.

Mix together the split peas, vegetables, mint and capers in a large bowl. Flour your hands and shape the mixture into 12 patties. Cover and chill until ready to cook.

Make the tzatziki by mixing the ingredients together in a bowl, cover and chill for 30 minutes before serving.

Heat a frying pan and spray with oil. Cook the patties, in batches if necessary, for 2 minutes on each side. Serve 3 patties per person, hot or cold, garnished with mint leaves, along with the tzatziki.

chicken tikka sticks & fennel raita

Calories per serving **179**
Serves **6**
Preparation time **20 minutes**,
    plus marinating and chilling
Cooking time **8–10 minutes**

1 **onion**, finely chopped
½–1 large **red** or **green
    chilli**, deseeded and finely
    chopped (to taste)
1.5 cm (¾ inch) piece of **fresh
    root ginger**, peeled and
    finely chopped
2 **garlic cloves**, finely chopped
150 ml (5 fl oz) **low-fat
    natural yogurt**
3 teaspoons **mild curry paste**
4 tablespoons chopped
    coriander
4 **skinless chicken breast
    fillers**, about 150 g (5 oz)
    each, cubed

Fennel raita
1 small **fennel bulb**, about
    200 g (7 oz)
200 ml (7 fl oz) **low-fat
    natural yogurt**
3 tablespoons chopped
    coriander
salt and **pepper**

Mix together the onion, chilli, ginger and garlic in
a non-metallic dish. Add the yogurt, curry paste and
coriander and stir together.

Add the cubed chicken to the yogurt mixture, mix to
coat, cover and leave to marinate in the refrigerator
for at least 2 hours.

Make the raita. Cut the core away from the fennel
and finely chop the remainder, including any green
tops. Mix the fennel with the yogurt and coriander and
season with salt and pepper. Spoon the raita into a
serving dish, cover and chill until needed.

Thread the chicken on to 12 bamboo skewers that
have been soaked in water for at least 20 minutes
and place them on a foil-lined grill rack. Cook under
a preheated grill for 8–10 minutes, turning once, until
browned and the chicken is cooked through. Serve
2 skewers per person with the raita.

For red pepper & almond chutney, to serve with the
skewers instead of the raita, place 75 g (3 oz) shop-
bought roasted peppers in a blender or food processor
with a handful of mint leaves, 1 chopped garlic clove
and ½ teaspoon chilli powder. Blend until smooth, then
add salt to taste and 1½ tablespoons toasted flaked
almonds. Pulse a couple of times to roughly crush the
almonds, then stir in 1 tablespoon chopped coriander.

turkey ragout

Calories per serving **190**
Serves **4**
Preparation time **10 minutes**
Cooking time **1 hour
50 minutes**

1 **turkey drumstick**, about
    625 g (1¼ lb)
2 **garlic cloves**, peeled
15 **baby onions** or **shallots**,
    peeled
3 **carrots**, diagonally sliced
300 ml (½ pint) **red wine**
a few **thyme sprigs**
2 **bay leaves**
2 tablespoons chopped
    flat leaf parsley
1 teaspoon **port wine jelly**
1 teaspoon **wholegrain
    mustard**
salt and **pepper**

Remove the skin from the turkey drumstick and
make a few cuts in the flesh. Finely slice 1 of the garlic
cloves and push the slivers into the slashes. Crush
the remaining garlic clove.

Transfer the drumstick to a large, flameproof casserole
or roasting tin with the onions or shallots, carrots,
crushed garlic, wine, thyme and bay leaves. Season well
with salt and pepper, cover and roast in a preheated
oven, 180°C (350°F), Gas Mark 4, for about 1¾ hours
or until the turkey is cooked through.

Remove the turkey and vegetables from the casserole
or roasting tin and keep hot. Bring the pan juices to
the boil on the hob, discarding the bay leaves. Add the
parsley, jelly and mustard and boil for 5 minutes until
slightly thickened. Season with salt and pepper. Carve
the turkey and serve with the vegetables and sauce in
4 serving bowls, accompanied by steamed new potatoes,
if liked (remembering to count the extra calories).

For spicy roast turkey with vegetables, prepare
the turkey drumstick as above, then rub with the juice
of 1 lemon and 2 tablespoons mild curry powder.
Toss the baby onions or shallots and chopped carrots
in 2 tablespoons olive oil and place in a roasting tin
with the turkey drumstick on top. Roast as above for
35 minutes, then add 2 cored, deseeded and chopped
red peppers, 1 large sweet potato, chopped, and
1 large courgette, thickly sliced. Baste the turkey with
any juices and roast for a further 1 hour or until the
turkey drumstick is cooked through. Carve the turkey
and serve with the vegetables and pan juices.

scallops with coriander yogurt

Calories per serving **217**
Serves **2**
Preparation time **15 minutes**
Cooking time **5 minutes**

150 ml (¼ pint) **low-fat
  natural yogurt**
2 tablespoons chopped
  coriander
finely grated rind and juice
  of 1 **lime**
2 teaspoons **sesame oil**
½ small **red onion**, finely
  chopped
15 g (½ oz) **fresh root ginger**,
  peeled and grated
1 **garlic clove**, crushed
2 teaspoons **caster sugar**
2 teaspoons **dark soy sauce**
1 tablespoon **water**
1 pointed **green pepper**,
  cored, deseeded and
  thinly sliced
200 g (7 oz) large **scallops**
rocket leaves, to serve

Mix together the yogurt, coriander and lime rind in
a small bowl, then transfer to a serving dish.

Heat half of the oil in a small frying pan and gently
fry the onion for 3 minutes until softened. Remove the
pan from the heat and add the ginger, garlic, sugar,
soy sauce, measurement water and lime juice.

Brush a griddle with the remaining oil. Add the green
pepper and scallops, cook the scallops for 1 minute on
each side until cooked through, and the pepper for a
little longer, if necessary.

Pile the pepper and scallops on to 2 serving plates
with the rocket. Heat the soy glaze through and spoon
it over the scallops. Serve with the yogurt sauce.

For squid & rocket salad with sweet soy glaze,
omit the scallops and green pepper. Make the yogurt
and coriander sauce as above and set aside. Heat
1 teaspoon groundnut oil in a large wok or frying pan
over a high heat. Add 200 g (7 oz) raw squid rings and
stir-fry for 1 minute before adding the onion, ginger and
garlic. Cook, stirring, for a further 1 minute, then add the
sugar, soy sauce, water and only 1 teaspoon sesame
oil. Stir for 30 seconds, then remove from the heat and
serve on a bed of rocket leaves with the yogurt and
coriander sauce on the side.

calves' liver with garlic mash

Calories per serving **393**
Serves **2**
Preparation time **10 minutes**
Cooking time **10–12 minutes**

350 g (11½ oz) **potatoes,**
    cubed
1 **garlic clove**, peeled
3 tablespoons **low-fat (less**
    than 3%) crème fraîche
½ tablespoon chopped **sage,**
    plus extra to garnish
1 tablespoon **plain flour**
2 slices of **calves' liver**, about
    150 g (5 oz) each
½ tablespoon **olive oil**
salt and **pepper**
gravy, to serve

Cook the potatoes and garlic in a saucepan of lightly salted boiling water for 10–12 minutes until tender, then drain. Return the potatoes and garlic to the pan and mash with the crème fraîche and sage. Season well with pepper.

Meanwhile, season the flour with salt and pepper, then press the pieces of liver into the seasoned flour to coat them all over. Heat the oil in a frying pan, add the liver and fry for 1–2 minutes on each side or until cooked to your liking.

Serve the liver hot with the garlic mash and gravy, garnished with extra chopped sage.

For calves' liver with garlic lentils, heat 1 tablespoon olive oil in a saucepan and cook 1 diced carrot, 2 diced celery sticks, 2 finely chopped garlic cloves and 1 diced onion for 3–4 minutes until softened. Add a drained 400 g (13 oz) can green lentils and cook for a further 4–5 minutes. Meanwhile, fry the liver as above. Stir the chopped sage into the lentils and serve with the liver.

thai mussel curry with ginger

Calories per serving **230**
Serves **4**
Preparation time **30 minutes**
Cooking time **13 minutes**

½–1 large **red chilli** (to taste)
2 **shallots**, quartered
1 **lemon grass stalk**
2.5 cm (1 inch) piece of
  fresh root ginger, peeled
  and chopped
1 tablespoon **sunflower oil**
400 ml (14 fl oz) can **reduced-
  fat coconut milk**
4–5 **kaffir lime leaves**
150 ml (¼ pint) **fish stock**
2 teaspoons **Thai fish sauce**
1.5 kg (3 lb) **fresh mussels**,
  soaked in cold water
1 small bunch of **coriander**,
  torn into pieces, to garnish

Halve the chilli and keep the seeds for extra heat,
if liked. Put the chilli, shallots and lemon grass into a
blender or food processor with the ginger and whiz
together until finely chopped.

Heat the oil in large, deep saucepan, add the finely
chopped ingredients and fry over a medium heat for
5 minutes, stirring until softened. Add the coconut milk,
kaffir lime leaves, fish stock and fish sauce and cook
for 3 minutes. Set aside.

Meanwhile, pick over the mussels and discard any that
are opened or have cracked shells. Scrub with a small
nailbrush, remove any barnacles and pull off any small,
hairy beards. Put them in a bowl of clean water and
leave until ready to cook.

Reheat the coconut milk mixture. Drain the mussels
and add to the mixture. Cover the pan with a lid and
cook for about 5 minutes until the mussel shells
have opened.

Spoon the mussels and the coconut sauce into 4 bowls,
discarding any mussels that have not opened. Garnish
with the coriander.

For Thai chicken & aubergine curry, prepare the
above recipe up to the end of the second step. Omit the
mussels. Pour in 250 ml (8 fl oz) chicken stock and bring
to the boil. Stir in 1 diced aubergine and 300 g (10 oz)
skinless chicken breast, cut into large chunks. Bring to
the boil again, cover and simmer for 12–15 minutes
until the chicken is cooked through and the aubergine
tender. Serve with a scattering of coriander.

pork skewers with coleslaw

Calories per serving **296**
Serves **4**
Preparation time **25 minutes**,
   plus marinating
Cooking time **7–10 minutes**

600 g (1¼ lb) **lean pork loin**,
   cubed

Barbecue marinade
2 tablespoons **muscovado
   sugar**
2 tablespoons **tomato ketchup**
2 tablespoons **dark soy sauce**
1 teaspoon **Chinese five-
   spice powder**
2 tablespoons **orange juice**

Coleslaw
1 tablespoon **red wine vinegar**
2 teaspoons **ready-made piri-
   piri sauce** or **marinade**
½ teaspoon **granulated sugar**
4–6 tablespoons **extra-light
   mayonnaise**
½ **red cabbage**, shredded
2 **carrots**, grated
2 **spring onions**, thinly sliced
salt and **pepper**

Mix together all the marinade ingredients in a large, non-metallic bowl until smooth. Add the pork and mix until well coated. Cover and leave to marinate at room temperature for 15 minutes.

Meanwhile, make the coleslaw. Mix together the vinegar, piri-piri sauce or marinade, sugar and mayonnaise in a small bowl. Toss together the cabbage, carrots and spring onions in a large bowl, then add the dressing and mix together until well combined. Season with salt and pepper and set aside.

Thread the pork on to 8 metal skewers and cook under a preheated grill for 7–10 minutes, turning occasionally, until cooked through and sticky. Serve 2 skewers per person with the coleslaw and steamed white rice, if liked (remembering to count the extra calories).

For sweet & spicy pork wraps, cut the pork into strips. Mix together the marinade ingredients as above, add the pork and mix until well coated. Cover and leave to marinate in the refrigerator for 30 minutes. Heat a griddle pan or heavy-based frying pan until hot, add the pork and cook for 6–8 minutes, turning frequently, until cooked through. Divide between 8 small flour tortillas. Cut 1 cucumber into thin matchsticks and divide between the tortillas along with 8 shredded spring onions. Roll up each tortilla around the filling and serve.

lamb & flageolet bean stew

Calories per serving **288**
Serves **4**
Preparation time **5 minutes**
Cooking time **1 hour**
  20 minutes

1 teaspoon **olive oil**
350 g (11½ oz) **lean lamb**,
  cubed
16 **pickling onions**, peeled
1 **garlic clove**, crushed
1 tablespoon **plain flour**
600 ml (1 pint) **lamb stock**
  (made with concentrated
  liquid stock)
200 g (7 oz) can **chopped
  tomatoes**
1 **bouquet garni**
2 x 400 g (13 oz) cans
  flageolet beans, drained
  and rinsed
250 g (8 oz) **cherry tomatoes**
pepper

Heat the oil in a flameproof casserole or saucepan, add
the lamb and fry for 3–4 minutes until browned all over.
Remove the lamb from the casserole and set aside.

Add the onions and garlic to the pan and fry for
4–5 minutes until the onions are beginning to brown.

Return the lamb and any juices to the pan, then stir
through the flour and add the stock, tomatoes, bouquet
garni and beans. Bring to the boil, stirring, then cover,
reduce the heat and simmer for 1 hour until the lamb
is just tender.

Add the cherry tomatoes to the dish and season well
with pepper. Simmer for a further 10 minutes, then
serve with steamed potatoes and green beans, if liked
(remembering to count the extra calories).

For pork & cider warming pot, replace the lamb with
350 g (11½ oz) lean pork tenderloin, cubed. Brown
as above and set aside. Cook the onions and garlic
as above, tip in the browned pork and stir in the flour.
Pour in 400 ml (14 fl oz) each of ham stock and cider,
instead of the lamb stock. Omit the canned tomatoes,
and add the bouquet garni and beans. Simmer, covered,
as above, adding 300 g (10 oz) cubed carrots to the
pan 30 minutes into cooking. Simmer for a further
30 minutes, omitting the cherry tomatoes. Remove from
the heat and stir in 2 tablespoons wholegrain mustard
and a handful of chopped flat leaf parsley.

chermoula tofu & roasted veg

Calories per serving **241**
Serves **4**
Preparation time **15 minutes**
Cooking time **1 hour**

25 g (1 oz) **coriander**,
   finely chopped
3 **garlic cloves**, chopped
1 teaspoon **cumin seeds**,
   lightly crushed
finely grated rind of **1 lemon**
½ teaspoon **dried chilli flakes**
4 tablespoons **olive oil**
250 g (8 oz) **tofu**
2 **red onions**, quartered
2 **courgettes**, thickly sliced
2 **red peppers**, cored,
   deseeded and sliced
2 **yellow peppers**, cored,
   deseeded and sliced
1 small **aubergine**,
   thickly sliced
salt

Mix together the coriander, garlic, cumin, lemon rind and chillies with 1 tablespoon of the oil and a little salt in a small bowl to make the chermoula.

Pat the tofu dry on kitchen paper and cut it in half. Cut each half horizontally into thin slices. Spread the chermoula generously over the slices. Set aside.

Scatter the vegetables in a roasting tin and drizzle with the remaining oil. Bake in a preheated oven, 200°C (400°F), Gas Mark 6, for about 45 minutes, until lightly browned, turning the ingredients once or twice during cooking.

Arrange the tofu slices over the vegetables, with the side spread with the chermoula uppermost, and bake for a further 10–15 minutes until the tofu is lightly coloured.

For chermoula tuna with tomato & courgette salad,

prepare the chermoula as above and rub it all over 4 fresh tuna steaks, about 125 g (4 oz) each. Leave to marinate while you prepare the salad. Thinly slice 4 courgettes, using a vegetable peeler, then place in a bowl and toss with 1 tablespoon olive oil. Heat a large, nonstick frying pan or griddle pan over a high heat, add the courgette strips and cook for 1–2 minutes on each side until golden. Slice 4 beef tomatoes and arrange on 4 plates with the cooked courgettes. Heat 2 tablespoons olive oil in the frying pan or griddle pan, add the tuna and cook for 1½ minutes on each side until browned on the outside but still pink in the centre. Serve with the salad, with the pan juices poured over, and lemon wedges for squeezing.

red mullet with baked tomatoes

Calories per serving **287**
Serves **4**
Preparation time **20 minutes**
Cooking time **18–20 minutes**

8 red mullet fillets, about
    100 g (3½ oz) each
finely grated rind of **1 lemon**
2 teaspoons **baby capers**,
    drained
2 **spring onions**, finely sliced
375 g (12 oz) mixed **red** and
    yellow cherry tomatoes
150 g (5 oz) **fine green
    beans**, trimmed
2 **garlic cloves**, finely chopped
50 g (2 oz) can **anchovy
    fillets**, drained and chopped
1 tablespoon **olive oil**
2 tablespoons **lemon juice**
salt and **pepper**

To garnish
2 tablespoons chopped
    parsley
8 **caperberries**

Tear off 4 large sheets of foil and line with nonstick baking paper. Place 2 fish fillets on each piece of baking paper, then scatter over the lemon rind, capers and spring onions and season with salt and pepper. Fold over the paper-lined foil and scrunch the edges together to seal. Place the parcels on a large baking sheet.

Put the tomatoes in an ovenproof dish with the beans, garlic, anchovies, oil and lemon juice. Season with salt and pepper and mix well. Bake in a preheated oven, 200°C (400°F), Gas Mark 6, for 10 minutes until the tomatoes and beans are tender.

Place the fish parcels next to the vegetables in the oven and bake for a further 8–10 minutes until the flesh flakes easily when pressed in the centre with a knife.

Spoon the vegetables on to 4 serving plates, then top each with 2 steamed fish fillets. Garnish with the chopped parsley and caperberries, and serve immediately.

For red mullet & tomato stew, heat 1 tablespoon olive oil in a saucepan, add the spring onions and garlic along with 1 trimmed and sliced fennel bulb and cook for 5 minutes until just softened. Add the tomatoes and 400 ml (14 fl oz) fish stock, bring to a simmer and cook for 15 minutes. Add 4 red mullet fillets, about 100 g (3½ oz) each, quartered, and 200 g (7 oz) cooked peeled prawns and cook for 3–4 minutes until the fish has turned opaque. Sprinkle in the chopped parsley and lemon juice, and serve with crusty bread.

lobster with shallots & vermouth

Calories per serving **275**
Serves **4**
Preparation time **1 hour**
Cooking time **10–11 minutes**

2 **cooked lobsters**, about
625–750 g (1¼–1½ lb) each
2 tablespoons **olive oil**
2 **shallots**, finely chopped
4 canned **anchovy fillets**,
drained and finely chopped
6 tablespoons **dry vermouth**
6 tablespoons **low-fat (less
than 3%) crème fraîche**
2–4 teaspoons **lemon juice**
(to taste)
pepper

To garnish
paprika
rocket leaves

Lay one lobster on its back. Cut in half, beginning at the head, down through the line between the claws, unfurling the tail as you cut until the lobster can be separated into two. Repeat with the second lobster. Take out the black, thread-like intestine that runs down the tail and the small whitish sac in the top of the head. Leave the greeny liver.

Twist off the big claws. Crack these open with poultry shears, a nutcracker, pestle or rolling pin. Peel away the shell and lift out the white meat, discarding the white, oval membrane in the centre of the claw. Twist off the small claws, taking care not to tear off body meat, and discard.

Scoop out the thick, white tail meat, slice and reserve it. Carefully remove the remaining lobster meat from the body, picking it over for stray pieces of shell and bone. Rinse the shells and put them on 4 serving plates.

Heat the oil in a large frying pan, add the shallots and fry gently for 5 minutes until softened and just beginning to colour. Mix in the anchovies, vermouth and pepper and cook for 2 minutes.

Add the lobster meat and crème fraîche and heat for 3–4 minutes. Stir in the lemon juice. Spoon into the shells, sprinkle with paprika and garnish with rocket.

For lobster & fennel salad, prepare the lobster flesh as above, cutting into large chunks, and then pan-fry in a hot frying pan in 1 tablespoon olive oil. Leave to cool while you thinly slice 2 fennel bulbs and 3 celery sticks. Whisk together the juice of 1 lemon, 4 tablespoons olive oil, 1 teaspoon Dijon mustard, 2 chopped tarragon sprigs and 1 crushed garlic clove. Toss with the lobster, fennel and celery, and serve on a bed of salad leaves.

chicken with spring vegetables

Calories per serving **370**
Serves **4**
Preparation time **15 minutes**,
    plus resting
Cooking time **about 1¼ hours**

1.5 kg (3 lb) **chicken**
about 1.5 litres (2½ pints)
    chicken stock
2 **shallots**, halved
2 **garlic cloves**, peeled
2 **parsley sprigs**
2 **marjoram sprigs**
2 **lemon thyme sprigs**
2 **carrots**, halved
1 **leek**, sliced
200 g (7 oz) **Tenderstem
    broccoli**
250 g (8 oz) **asparagus**,
    trimmed
½ **Savoy cabbage**, shredded

Put the chicken in a large saucepan and pour over enough stock to just cover the chicken. Add the shallots, garlic, herbs, carrots and leek to the pan and bring to the boil over a medium-high heat, then reduce the heat and simmer gently for 1 hour or until the chicken is falling away from the bones.

Add the remaining vegetables to the pan and simmer for a further 6–8 minutes until the vegetables are cooked.

Turn off the heat and leave to rest for 5–10 minutes. Remove the skin from the chicken, then divide the chicken between 4 deep serving bowls with the vegetables, with spoonfuls of the broth ladled over. Serve with hunks of crusty bread, if liked (remember to count the extra calories).

For grilled chicken with spring vegetables, cook 4 skinless chicken breast fillets, about 125 g (4 oz) each, under a preheated grill for 8–10 minutes on each side or until cooked through. Meanwhile, put the broccoli, asparagus and Savoy cabbage in the top of a steamer, cover and cook for a few minutes until just tender. Divide the vegetables between 4 warmed plates, top with the grilled and sliced chicken and scatter with chopped parsley and thyme, then drizzle lightly with extra-virgin olive oil.

thai beef & mixed pepper stir-fry

Calories per serving **255**
Serves **4**
Preparation time **15 minutes**
Cooking time **8–10 minutes**

500 g (1 lb) **lean beef fillet**
1 tablespoon **sesame oil**
1 **garlic clove**, finely chopped
1 **lemon grass stalk**, finely
  shredded
2.5 cm (1 inch) piece of **fresh
  root ginger**, peeled and
  finely chopped
1 **red pepper**, cored,
  deseeded and thickly sliced
1 **green pepper**, cored,
  deseeded and thickly sliced
1 **onion**, thickly sliced
2 tablespoons **lime juice**
pepper
coriander leaves, to garnish

Cut the beef across the grain into long, thin strips.

Heat the oil in a wok or large frying pan over a high heat.
Add the garlic and stir-fry for 1 minute. Add the beef and
stir-fry for 2–3 minutes until lightly coloured. Stir in the
lemon grass and ginger and remove the pan from the
heat. Remove the beef from the pan and set aside.

Add the peppers and onion to the pan and stir-fry for
2–3 minutes until the onions are just turning golden
brown and are slightly softened.

Return the beef to the pan, stir in the lime juice and
season to taste with pepper. Serve garnished with
coriander leaves and accompanied by steamed white
rice, if liked (remembering to count the extra calories).

For marinated tofu & vegetable stir-fry, replace the
beef with 400 g (13 oz) tofu, patted dry with kitchen
paper and cut into strips. Mix together 3 tablespoons
soy sauce, 2 teaspoons clear honey and 1 teaspoon
Dijon mustard in a bowl, add the tofu and toss until well
coated. Cover and leave to marinate for 30 minutes.
Cook the stir-fry as above, adding the tofu at the end
of cooking, along with 50 g (2 oz) bean sprouts.

prawns with tamarind & lime

Calories per serving **122**
Serves **6**
Preparation time **5 minutes**
Cooking time **10 minutes**

1 kg (2 lb) large **raw
langoustine prawns** in their
shells (thawed if frozen)
2 tablespoons **olive oil**
1 large **onion**, chopped
3–4 **garlic cloves**, finely
chopped
4 cm (1½ inch) piece of **fresh
root ginger**, peeled and
finely chopped
2 teaspoons **tamarind paste**
juice of **2 limes**
300 ml (½ pint) **fish stock**
1 small bunch of **coriander**,
torn into pieces, to garnish
lime wedges, to serve

Heat the oil in a large saucepan or wok, add the onion
and fry the prawns for 5 minutes until just beginning
to brown.

Stir in the garlic, ginger and tamarind paste, then mix
in the lime juice and stock.

Bring the stock to the boil, add the prawns and cook,
stirring, for 5 minutes until the prawns are bright pink.
Spoon into 6 bowls and serve garnished with the torn
coriander leaves and lime wedges.

For prawns with tomato & coconut, brown the
onions as above. Add the prawns, garlic and ginger
and fry until the prawns turn pink, then add the lime
juice, 2 teaspoons tamarind paste, 100 ml (3½ fl oz)
reduced-fat coconut milk and 3 tomatoes, deseeded
and finely chopped. Omit the stock. Bring to the boil,
then reduce the heat and simmer for 2 minutes.
Serve with the coriander and lime garnish.

wild mushroom stroganoff

Calories per serving **206**
Serves **4**
Preparation time **15 minutes**
Cooking time **15–16 minutes**

25 g (1 oz) **butter**

1 tablespoon **olive oil**

1 **onion**, sliced

400 g (13 oz) **chestnut cup mushrooms**, sliced

2 **garlic cloves**, finely chopped

2 teaspoons **paprika**, plus extra to garnish

6 tablespoons **vodka**

400 ml (14 fl oz) **Vegetable Stock** (see page 48)

generous pinch of **ground cinnamon**

generous pinch of **ground mace**

150 g (5 oz) **wild mushrooms**, large ones sliced

6 tablespoons **low-fat (less than 3%) crème fraîche**

salt and **pepper**

chopped **parsley**, to garnish

Heat the butter and oil in a frying pan, add the onion and fry for 5 minutes until lightly browned. Stir in the cup mushrooms and garlic and cook for 4 minutes. Stir in the paprika and cook for 1 minute.

Pour in the vodka. When it is bubbling, flame with a match and stand well back. Once the flames have subsided, stir in the stock, cinnamon and mace and season with salt and pepper. Simmer for 3–4 minutes.

Add the wild mushrooms and cook for 2 minutes. Stir in 2 tablespoons of the crème fraîche.

Spoon the stroganoff on to 4 serving plates and top with spoonfuls of the remaining crème fraîche, a sprinkling of paprika and a little parsley. Serve with sweet potato mash, if liked (remembering to count the extra calories).

For wild mushroom risotto, heat the butter and olive oil in a frying pan and sauté the chopped onion, and wild mushrooms for 4–5 minutes until golden. Add the garlic and cook for 1 minute, then pour in 125 ml (4 fl oz) white wine and 200 g (7 oz) risotto rice and stir well. Add up to 1 litre (1¾ pints) hot vegetable stock to the pan one ladleful at a time, stirring and allowing the liquid to be absorbed before adding more, and cook until the rice is al dente – about 20 minutes. Season with salt and pepper and serve with a sprinkling of grated Parmesan cheese and chopped parsley.

scallops with white bean purée

Calories per serving **293**
Serves **4**
Preparation time **10 minutes**
Cooking time **20 minutes**

2 x 400 g (13 oz) cans
    cannellini beans, drained
    and rinsed
2 **garlic cloves**
200 ml (7 fl oz) **Vegetable
    Stock** (see page 48)
2 tablespoons chopped
    parsley
2 teaspoons **olive oil**
16 **baby leeks**
3 tablespoons **water**
16 large **scallops**
parsley sprigs, to garnish

Place the beans, garlic and stock in a saucepan and bring to the boil, then reduce the heat and simmer for 10 minutes. Remove from the heat, drain off any excess liquid, then mash with a potato masher and stir in the parsley. Keep warm.

Heat half the oil in a nonstick frying pan, add the leeks and fry for 2 minutes, then add the measurement water. Cover and simmer for 5–6 minutes until tender.

Meanwhile, heat the remaining oil in a small frying pan, add the scallops and fry for 1 minute on each side until just cooked through. Serve with the white bean purée and leeks and garnish with parsley sprigs.

For Parma ham wrapped scallops with minty pea purée, make the purée as above, replacing the beans with 300 g (10 oz) frozen and thawed peas, and using mint instead of parsley. Remove the fat from 8 slices of Parma ham and cut them in half widthways. Wrap a strip of ham around each scallop and season with salt and pepper. Omit the leeks. Heat all the oil in a large nonstick frying pan, add the scallops and cook for 2 minutes on each side until just cooked through. Serve immediately with the pea purée.

lime & ginger prawn coleslaw

Calories per serving **143**
Serves **2**
Preparation time **15 minutes**
Cooking time **2–3 minutes**

¼ **Chinese cabbage** or
  pointed spring cabbage,
  thinly shredded
1 **carrot**, coarsely grated
100 g (3½ oz) **bean sprouts**
½ small bunch of **coriander**,
  finely chopped
1 **spring onion**, thinly sliced
125 g (4 oz) **raw peeled
  king prawns**
1 teaspoon **Chinese five-
  spice powder**
½ tablespoon **groundnut oil**
lime wedges, to serve

Dressing
1 teaspoon peeled and finely
  grated **fresh root ginger**
1 tablespoon **lime juice**
½ teaspoon **palm sugar** or
  soft light brown sugar
1 tablespoon **light soy sauce**
½ tablespoon **groundnut oil**

Toss together the cabbage, carrot, bean sprouts, coriander and spring onion in a large bowl and set aside.

Make the dressing by placing all the ingredients in a screw-top jar, adding the lid and shaking until well combined. Set aside.

Mix together the prawns and Chinese five-spice powder in a bowl until the prawns are well coated. Heat the oil in a wok or frying pan over a medium-high heat, add the prawns and stir-fry for 2–3 minutes until they turn pink and are cooked through. Remove from the pan and drain on kitchen paper.

Pour the dressing over the vegetables and toss together, then heap the coleslaw on 2 serving plates. Scatter over the prawns and serve with lime wedges.

For lime & ginger prawn stir-fry, heat 1 tablespoon groundnut oil in a wok or frying pan over a medium-high heat, add the ginger, Chinese five-spice powder and spring onion and stir-fry for 1 minute. Add the cabbage, carrot and bean sprouts and stir-fry for 1–2 minutes, then stir in the prawns and stir-fry as above. Toss with the lime juice, soy sauce and chopped coriander and serve immediately, with boiled rice, if liked.

spicy aubergine curry

Calories per serving **231**
Serves **4**
Preparation time **15 minutes**,
   plus cooling
Cooking time **20 minutes**

1 teaspoon **cumin seeds**
4 teaspoons **coriander seeds**
1 teaspoon **cayenne pepper**
2 **green chillies**, deseeded
   and sliced
½ teaspoon **ground turmeric**
4 **garlic cloves**, crushed
2.5 cm (1 inch) piece of
   fresh root ginger, peeled
   and grated
300 ml (½ pint) **warm water**
400 g (13 oz) can **reduced-fat
   coconut milk**
1 tablespoon **tamarind paste**
1 large **aubergine**, thinly sliced
   lengthways
salt and **pepper**
4 **mini plain naan breads**,
   to serve

Dry-fry the cumin and coriander seeds in a small, nonstick frying pan for a few minutes until aromatic and toasted. Leave to cool, then crush together.

Mix together the crushed seeds, cayenne, chillies, turmeric, garlic, ginger and the measurement water in a large saucepan and simmer for 10 minutes until thickened. Season with salt and pepper, then stir in the coconut milk and tamarind paste.

Arrange the aubergine slices on a foil-lined grill rack and brush the tops with some of the curry sauce. Cook under a preheated hot grill until golden.

Stir the aubergine slices into the curry sauce. Serve hot with mini plain naan breads.

asian steamed chicken salad

Calories per serving **273**
Serves **2**
Preparation time **15 minutes**,
    plus cooling
Cooking time **8–10 minutes**

2 **skinless chicken breast
    fillets**, about 150 g
    (5 oz) each
¼ small **Chinese cabbage**,
    finely shredded
½ **large carrot**, grated
125 g (4 oz) **bean sprouts**
handful of **coriander**,
    finely chopped
handful of **mint**, finely chopped
½ **red chilli**, deseeded and
    finely sliced (optional)

Dressing
40 ml (1½ fl oz) **sunflower oil**
juice of **1 lime**
¾ tablespoon **Thai fish sauce**
1½ tablespoons **light
    soy sauce**
½ tablespoon peeled and
    finely chopped **fresh
    root ginger**

Put the chicken in the top of a steamer, cover and
cook for about 8 minutes or until the chicken is cooked
through. Alternatively, poach the chicken in a pan of
simmering water for 8–10 minutes until cooked through
and tender. Remove from the pan and leave until cool
enough to handle.

Meanwhile, make the dressing by placing all the
ingredients in a screw-top jar, adding the lid and shaking
until well combined.

Cut or tear the cooked chicken into strips and mix
with 1 tablespoon of the dressing in a bowl. Leave to
cool completely.

Toss together all the vegetables, herbs and chilli, if
using, in a large bowl, then divide between 2 serving
plates. Scatter over the cold chicken and serve
immediately with the remaining dressing.

For Asian chicken stir-fry, heat 1 tablespoon
sunflower oil in a wok over a high heat, add the
chicken, cut into strips, chilli and ginger and stir-fry for
2–3 minutes until the chicken is browned. Add 1 carrot,
cut into matchsticks, and stir-fry for 1 minute, then
add the cabbage and bean sprouts and stir-fry for a
further 2 minutes. Toss in the lime juice, Thai fish sauce
and soy sauce, then finally the chopped herbs. Serve
immediately, with boiled rice, if liked.

seafood zarzuela

Calories per serving **240**
Serves **4**
Preparation time **30 minutes**
Cooking time **25 minutes**

500 g (1 lb) **tomatoes**
1 tablespoon **olive oil**
1 large **onion**, finely chopped
2 **garlic cloves**, finely chopped
½ teaspoon **pimentón**
(smoked paprika)
1 **red pepper**, cored,
deseeded and diced
200 ml (7 fl oz) **fish stock**
150 ml (¼ pint) **dry white
wine**
2 large pinches of **saffron
threads**
4 small **bay leaves**
500 g (1 lb) **fresh mussels**,
soaked in cold water
200 g (7 oz) **raw squid**,
cleaned and rinsed in
cold water
375 g (12 oz) **skinless
cod loin**, cubed
salt and **pepper**

Put the tomatoes in a large saucepan or heatproof bowl and pour over enough boiling water to cover, then leave for about 1 minute. Drain and cool in a bowl of ice-cold water, then drain again. Skin the tomatoes and roughly chop the flesh.

Heat the oil in a large saucepan, add the onion and fry for 5 minutes until softened and just beginning to brown. Stir in the garlic and pimentón and cook, stirring, for a further 1 minute.

Stir in the tomatoes, red pepper, stock, wine and saffron. Add the bay leaves, season with salt and pepper and bring to the boil. Cover and simmer gently for 10 minutes, then remove the pan from the heat and set aside.

Meanwhile, pick over the mussels and discard any that are opened or have cracked shells. Scrub with a small nailbrush, remove any barnacles and pull off any small, hairy beards. Put them in a bowl of clean water and leave until ready to cook. Separate the squid tubes from the tentacles, then slice the tubes.

Reheat the tomato sauce if necessary, add the cod and the sliced squid and cook for 2 minutes. Drain the mussels and add to the pan, cover and cook for 4 minutes. Add the squid tentacles and cook for a further 2 minutes until the fish is cooked through and all the mussel shells have opened. Gently stir, then serve, discarding any mussels that have not opened.

desserts

orangey baked nectarines

Calories per serving **161**
Serves **2**
Preparation time **10 minutes**
Cooking time **18–20 minutes**

25 ml (1 fl oz) **orange liqueur,**
  such as Cointreau
½ teaspoon **vanilla bean**
  paste or **extract**
finely grated rind of ¼ **orange**
1 tablespoon **clear honey**
2 firm ripe **nectarines,** halved
  and stoned
75 ml (3 fl oz) **0% fat Greek**
  yogurt with honey, to serve

Put the liqueur, vanilla bean paste or extract, orange rind and honey in a bowl and stir until well combined.

Arrange the nectarines, cut-side up, in an ovenproof dish, then drizzle over the liqueur mixture. Bake in a preheated oven, 180°C (350°F), Gas Mark 4, for 18–20 minutes until tender.

Divide the nectarines between 2 serving bowls and serve with the yogurt, drizzled with the pan juices.

For amaretti baked nectarines, arrange the nectarine halves in an ovenproof dish as above, then crumble 1 amaretti biscuit into each one and drizzle each with 1 teaspoon maple syrup. Bake and then serve with the yogurt as above.

strawberry roulade

Calories per serving **177**
Serves **8**
Preparation time **30 minutes**,
   plus cooling
Cooking time **8 minutes**

3 **eggs**
125 g (4 oz) **caster sugar**
125 g (4 oz) **plain flour**, sifted
1 tablespoon **hot water**
500 g (1 lb) fresh or frozen,
   thawed, drained and
   quartered **strawberries**,
   or 425 g (14 oz) can
   strawberries in natural
   juice, drained and quartered
200 ml (7 fl oz) **fat-free**
   natural fromage frais or
   low-fat natural yogurt
icing sugar, for dusting

Lightly grease a 33 x 23 cm (13 x 9 inch) Swiss roll tin. Line with a single sheet of greaseproof paper to come about 1 cm (½ inch) above the sides of the tin. Lightly grease the paper.

Whisk the eggs and sugar in a large bowl over a saucepan of hot water until pale and thick. Fold the flour into the egg mixture with the measurement water. Pour the batter into the prepared tin and bake in a preheated oven, 220°C (425°F), Gas Mark 7, for 8 minutes until golden and set.

Meanwhile, place a sheet of greaseproof paper 2.5 cm (1 inch) larger all round than the Swiss roll tin on a clean, damp tea towel. Once cooked, immediately turn out the Swiss roll face down on to the paper. Carefully peel off the lining paper. Roll the sponge up tightly with the new greaseproof paper inside. Wrap the tea towel around the outside and place on a wire rack until cool, then unroll carefully.

Add half the strawberries to the fromage frais or yogurt and spread over the sponge. Roll the sponge up again and trim the ends. Dust with icing sugar and decorate with a few strawberries. Purée the remaining strawberries in a food processor or blender and serve as a sauce with the roll.

For vanilla & jam roll, make the batter as above, folding in ½ teaspoon vanilla extract before baking. Bake, then roll, wrap and cool as above. Lightly heat 150 g (5 oz) raspberry jam and spread it over the sponge. Roll the sponge up again, trim the ends and dust with icing sugar.

caramel pear & marzipan tart

Calories per serving **268**
Serves **8**
Preparation time **10 minutes**,
  plus cooling
Cooking time **45 minutes**

50 g (2 oz) **unsalted butter**
50 g (2 oz) **soft light
  brown sugar**
25 g (1 oz) **marzipan**
6 ripe **pears**, peeled, halved
  and cored
250 g (8 oz) **ready-made
  shortcrust pastry**

Place the butter and sugar in a 22 cm (9 inch) fixed-bottomed cake tin. Place over a medium heat and cook for about 5 minutes, stirring continuously, until golden. Remove from the heat.

Stuff a little marzipan into the cavity of each pear half, then carefully arrange them cut-side up in the tin.

Roll out the pastry on a lightly floured surface to the size of the tin, then place over the top of the pears and press down all around them. Bake in a preheated oven, 190°C (375°F), Gas Mark 5, for about 40 minutes until the pastry is golden and the juices are bubbling.

Leave to cool in the tin for 10 minutes, then invert on to a large plate, cut into 8 wedges and serve with a little ice cream, if liked (remembering to count the extra calories).

For pear, blackberry & marzipan tart, roll out the pastry as above and place it on a baking sheet. Core and chop 4 pears and combine in a bowl with the soft light brown sugar, marzipan and 150 g (5 oz) blackberries. Omit the butter. Place the fruit in the centre of the pastry round, leaving a 5 cm (2 inch) rim, then lift the rim up over the edges of the fruit to make a tart. Brush the pastry with 1 tablespoon skimmed milk and dust with 1 tablespoon caster sugar. Bake as above and serve warm.

ricotta, plum & almond cake

Calories per serving **150**
Serves **6**
Preparation time **30 minutes,**
  plus cooling and chilling
Cooking time **35–40 minutes**

500 g (1 lb) sweet, ripe **red**
  plums, stoned and quartered
250 g (8 oz) **ricotta cheese**
4–5 tablespoons **granulated**
  sweetener
3 **eggs,** separated
¼ teaspoon **almond extract**
4 teaspoons **flaked almonds**
2 tablespoons **water**
1 tablespoon **icing sugar,**
  sifted

Arrange half the plums randomly over the base of a buttered and base-lined 20 cm (8 inch) springform tin.

Mix together the ricotta, 4 tablespoons of the sweetener, the egg yolks and almond extract in a bowl until smooth.

Whisk the egg whites in a second clean bowl until stiff peaks form. Fold into the ricotta mixture, then spoon over the plums. Sprinkle with the flaked almonds and bake in a preheated oven, 160°C (325°F), Gas Mark 3, for 30–35 minutes until the cake is risen, golden and the centre is just set. Check after 20 minutes and cover the top with foil if the almonds are browning too quickly.

Turn off the oven and leave the cake to cool with the door ajar for 15 minutes, then chill well.

Meanwhile, cook the remaining plums with the measurement water in a covered saucepan for 5 minutes until soft. Purée until smooth, mix in the remaining sweetener, if needed, then pour into a small jug.

Remove the tin and lining paper and transfer the cake to a serving plate. Dust the top with the icing sugar and serve, cut into 6 wedges, with the sauce.

For roasted almond plums with honeyed ricotta, mix together 4 tablespoons oats and 2 tablespoons plain flour in a bowl, add 40 g (1½ oz) diced butter and rub in with the fingertips until the mixture resembles breadcrumbs. Stir in ½ tablespoon soft light brown sugar and the flaked almonds. Place the plums in a baking tray and spoon the crumble over the top of each. Bake in a preheated oven, 200°C (400°F), Gas Mark 6, for 12–15 minutes. Serve with a dollop of ricotta and a drizzle of honey.

chocolate & chestnut roulade

Calories per serving **215**
Serves **8**
Preparation time **15 minutes**,
  plus cooling and chilling
Cooking time **20 minutes**

6 **eggs**, separated
125 g (4 oz) **caster sugar**
2 tablespoons **cocoa powder**
150 ml (¼ pint) **whipping
  cream**
100 g (3½ oz) **chestnut
  purée** or **sweetened
  chestnut spread**
icing sugar, for dusting

Grease and line a 29 x 18 cm (11½ x 7 inch) Swiss roll tin. Whisk the egg whites in a large clean bowl until they form soft peaks. Put the egg yolks and sugar in a separate bowl and whisk together until thick and pale. Fold in the cocoa powder and the egg whites, then tip into the prepared tin.

Bake in a preheated oven, 180°C (350°F), Gas Mark 4, for 20 minutes. Leave to cool in the tin, then tip out on to a piece of greaseproof paper that has been dusted with icing sugar.

Pour the cream into a large clean bowl and whisk until it forms soft peaks. Fold the chestnut purée or spread into the cream, then smooth the mixture over the roulade.

Using the greaseproof paper to help you, carefully roll up the roulade from one short end and lift it gently on to a serving dish (do not worry if it cracks). Dust with icing sugar. Chill until needed and eat on the day it is made.

For chocolate orange roulade, prepare and bake the sponge cake as above. Whip the cream for the filling, then fold in 1 tablespoon marmalade and the finely grated rind of 1 orange. Omit the chestnut purée or spread. Spread the filling over the cake and roll up as above. Serve dusted with sifted icing sugar.

white chocolate mousse

Calories per serving **202**
Serves **8**
Preparation time **15 minutes**,
  plus chilling

200 g (7 oz) **white chocolate,**
  chopped
4 tablespoons **skimmed milk**
12 **cardamom pods**
200 g (7 oz) **silken tofu**
50 g (2 oz) **caster sugar**
1 **egg white**
240 g (7¾ oz) **low-fat (less
  than 3%) crème fraîche,**
  to serve
cocoa powder, for dusting

Put the chocolate and milk in a heatproof bowl and melt over a saucepan of gently simmering water. To release the cardamom seeds, crush the pods using a pestle and mortar. Discard the pods and crush the seeds finely.

Place the cardamom pods and tofu in a food processor with half of the sugar and blend well to a smooth paste. Turn the mixture into a large bowl.

Whisk the egg white in a thoroughly clean bowl until it forms peaks. Gradually whisk in the remaining sugar.

Beat the melted chocolate mixture into the tofu mixture until completely combined. Using a large metal spoon, fold in the egg white. Spoon the mousse into 8 small coffee cups or glasses and chill for at least 1 hour. Serve topped with spoonfuls of crème fraîche and a light dusting of cocoa powder.

For white chocolate & amaretto pots, make the mousse mixture as above, omitting the cardamom and adding 2 tablespoons amaretto when blending the tofu. Complete the recipe and chill as above. Serve with fresh raspberries instead of the crème fraîche and cocoa.

passion fruit panna cotta

Calories per serving **144**
Serves **2**
Preparation time **15 minutes**,
   plus cooling and chilling
Cooking time **5 minutes**

1 **gelatine leaf**
4 **passion fruit**
100 g (3½ oz) **half-fat
   crème fraîche**
50 ml (2 fl oz) **0% fat
   Greek yogurt**
50 ml (2 fl oz) **water**
½ teaspoon **caster sugar**
½ **vanilla pod**, split
   lengthways

Soak the gelatine leaf in a bowl of cold water for a
few minutes until softened.

Meanwhile, working over a bowl to catch the juice,
halve the passion fruit, remove the seeds and reserve
for decoration. Mix the crème fraîche and yogurt into
the passion fruit juice in the bowl.

Put the measurement water in a saucepan with the
sugar. Scrape the seeds from the vanilla pod into the pan,
then heat gently, stirring, until the sugar has dissolved.

Drain the gelatine and add to the pan, then leave to cool.

Mix the gelatine mixture into the crème fraîche mixture,
then pour into 2 ramekins or moulds. Cover and chill
for 6 hours or until set. Turn the panna cotta out of
the ramekins or moulds on to serving plates by briefly
immersing their bases in hot water. Spoon over the
reserved passion fruit seeds and serve.

chocolate & raspberry soufflés

Calories per serving **287**
Serves **4**
Preparation time **10 minutes**
Cooking time **15–18 minutes**

100 g (3½ oz) **plain dark chocolate**, broken into squares
3 **eggs**, separated
50 g (2 oz) **self-raising flour**, sifted
40 g (1½ oz) **caster sugar**
150 g (5 oz) **raspberries**
icing sugar, for dusting

Put the chocolate in a heatproof bowl and melt over a saucepan of gently simmering water.

Place the melted chocolate in a large bowl and whisk in the egg yolks. Fold in the flour.

Whisk the egg whites and caster sugar in a medium clean bowl until they form soft peaks. Beat a spoonful of the egg whites into the chocolate mixture to loosen it up before gently folding in the rest.

Divide the raspberries between 4 lightly greased ramekins, pour over the chocolate mixture, then bake in a preheated oven, 190°C (375°F), Gas Mark 5, for 12–15 minutes until the soufflés have risen.

Dust with icing sugar and serve immediately.

For chocolate & coffee soufflés, stir 2 teaspoons instant coffee granules into the hot melted chocolate until it dissolves. Bake the soufflés as above, omitting the raspberries. Make a cappuccino cream to serve with the soufflés by folding 2 tablespoons sweetened strong black coffee into 100 g (3½ oz) low-fat (less than 3%) crème fraîche. Serve the soufflés straight out of the oven with a dollop of the cream.

brûlée vanilla cheesecake

Calories per serving **160**
Serves **8**
Preparation time **30 minutes**,
  plus cooling and chilling
Cooking time **30–35 minutes**

butter, for greasing
3 x 200 g (7 oz) packets
  low-fat cream cheese
6 tablespoons **granulated
  sweetener**
1½ teaspoons **vanilla extract**
finely grated rind of ½ **orange**
4 **eggs**, separated
1 tablespoon **icing sugar**,
  sifted
3 **oranges**, peeled and cut
  into segments, to serve

Lightly grease a 20 cm (8 inch) springform tin. Mix together the cream cheese, sweetener, vanilla extract, orange rind and egg yolks in a bowl until smooth.

Whisk the egg whites in a clean large bowl until soft peaks form, then fold a large spoonful into the cheese mixture to loosen it. Add the remaining egg whites and fold them in gently.

Pour the mixture into the prepared tin and level the surface. Bake in a preheated oven, 160°C (325°F), Gas Mark 3, for 30–35 minutes until well risen, golden brown and just set in the centre.

Turn off the oven and leave the cheesecake to cool for 15 minutes with the door slightly ajar. Remove from the oven, leave to cool, then chill for 4 hours. (The cheesecake will sink slightly as it cools.)

Run a knife around the cheesecake, loosen the tin and transfer to a serving plate. Dust the top with the icing sugar and caramelize the sugar with a cook's blowtorch. Serve within 30 minutes, while the sugar topping is still hard and brittle. Cut into 8 wedges and arrange on plates with the orange segments.

For lemon drizzle cheesecake, make the cheesecake as above, using the finely grated rind of 1 lemon in place of the orange rind. When the cheesecake has been chilled and removed from the tin, mix 3 tablespoons sifted icing sugar with enough juice squeezed from the lemon to give a runny syrup. Spoon over the cheesecake and sprinkle with the grated rind of another lemon.

orange, rhubarb & ginger slump

Calories per serving **256**
Serves **6**
Preparation time **10 minutes**
Cooking time **20–25 minutes**

750 g (1½ lb) **rhubarb**,
    chopped into 1.5 cm
    (¾ inch) pieces
½ teaspoon **ground ginger**
grated rind and juice of
    1 orange
50 g (2 oz) **golden caster
    sugar**
4 tablespoons **reduced-fat
    mascarpone cheese**
175 g (6 oz) **self-raising
    flour**, sifted
50 g (2 oz) **unsalted butter**,
    cut into small pieces
grated rind of ½ **lemon**
6 tablespoons **skimmed milk**

Put the rhubarb, ginger, orange rind and juice and half
the sugar in a saucepan. Bring to the boil, then reduce
the heat and simmer gently for 5–6 minutes until the
rhubarb is just tender.

Transfer the rhubarb to an ovenproof dish and spoon
over dollops of mascarpone.

Place the flour in a bowl. Add the butter and rub in
with the fingertips until the mixture resembles fine
breadcrumbs. Quickly stir through the remaining sugar,
the lemon rind and milk until combined. Place spoonfuls
of the mixture over the rhubarb and mascarpone.

Bake in a preheated oven, 200°C (400°F), Gas Mark 6,
for 12–15 minutes until golden and bubbling. Serve
with low-fat custard, if liked (remembering to count the
extra calories).

For plum & apple slump, replace the rhubarb with
500 g (1 lb) plums, stoned and cut into 1.5 cm (¾ inch)
pieces, and 1 dessert apple, cored and cubed. Cook
with the ginger, sugar and orange until just tender, then
transfer to an ovenproof dish. Spoon over 4 tablespoons
low-fat (less than 3%) crème fraîche instead of the
mascarpone, then continue as above.

champagne granita

Calories per serving **80**

Serves **6**

Preparation time **25 minutes**,
  plus cooling and freezing

40 g (1½ oz) **light brown
  sugar**

150 ml (¼ pint) **boiling water**

375 ml (13 fl oz) **medium-dry
  champagne**

150 g (5 oz) **raspberries**

Stir the sugar into the measurement water until it has
dissolved, then leave to cool.

Mix together the sugar syrup and champagne. Pour it
into a shallow, nonstick baking tin so that it is no more
than 2.5 cm (1 inch) deep.

Freeze the mixture for 2 hours until it is mushy, then
break up the ice crystals with a fork. Return the mixture
to the freezer for 2 more hours, beating every 30 minutes
until it has formed fine, icy flakes.

Spoon the granita into 6 elegant glasses and top with
the raspberries.

For pink grapefruit & ginger granita, grate a 2.5 cm
(1 inch) piece of peeled fresh root ginger into the
boiling water and sugar and stir until the sugar has
dissolved. Set aside for 30 minutes before mixing the
ginger sugar syrup into 350 ml (12 fl oz) fresh pink
grapefruit juice, instead of the champagne. Complete
the recipe as above, omitting the raspberries.

rhubarb & ginger parfait

Calories per serving **110**

Serves **6**

Preparation time **20 minutes**, plus soaking, cooling and chilling

Cooking time **8–9 minutes**

400 g (13 oz) **trimmed forced rhubarb**, sliced

2.5 cm (1 inch) piece of **fresh root ginger**, peeled and finely chopped

5 tablespoons **water**

3 teaspoons **powdered gelatine**

4 **egg yolks**

6 tablespoons **granulated sweetener**

200 ml (7 fl oz) **skimmed milk**

2 **egg whites**

125 g (4 oz) **low-fat (less than 3%) crème fraîche**

a few drops of **pink food colouring** (optional)

orange rind, to decorate

Put the rhubarb pieces in a saucepan with the ginger and 2 tablespoons of the water. Cover and simmer for 5 minutes until tender yet still bright pink. Mash or purée.

Put the remaining water in a small bowl and sprinkle over the gelatine, making sure that all the powder is absorbed by the water. Leave to soak for 5 minutes.

Whisk the egg yolks and sweetener until just mixed. Pour the milk into a small saucepan and bring just to the boil. Gradually whisk the milk into the egg yolks, then pour the mixture back into the saucepan. Slowly bring the custard almost to the boil, stirring continuously, until it coats the back of the spoon. Do not allow the custard to boil or the eggs will curdle.

Remove the pan from the heat and stir in the gelatine until it has dissolved. Pour into a bowl, stir in the cooked rhubarb and leave to cool.

Whisk the egg whites until stiff, moist peaks form. Fold the crème fraîche and a few drops of colouring, if used, into the cooled custard, then fold in the whisked whites. Spoon into 6 glasses and chill for 4 hours until lightly set. Decorate with orange rind just before serving.

For rhubarb & ginger crumbles, cook the rhubarb and ginger as above, adding 3 tablespoons of the sweetener, but do not mash or purée. Divide between 4 ramekins on a baking sheet. Sift 175 g (6 oz) plain flour into a bowl, add 75 g (3 oz) diced butter and rub in until resembling breadcrumbs. Stir in 2 tablespoons dark muscovado sugar and the grated rind of 1 orange. Sprinkle over the rhubarb mixture, then bake in a preheated oven, 190°C (375°F), Gas Mark 5, for 20–25 minutes until golden.

cherry & nectarine pavlova

Calories per serving **245**
Serves **6**
Preparation time **20 minutes**,
  plus cooling
Cooking time **1 hour**

3 **egg whites**
175 g (6 oz) **caster sugar**
1 teaspoon **strong black
  coffee**
250 g (8 oz) **fat-free natural
  fromage frais**
125 g (4 oz) **cherries**
125 g (4 oz) **nectarines**,
  stoned and cut into chunks

Whisk the egg whites in a clean bowl until they form stiff peaks. Fold in 1 tablespoon of the sugar, then gradually whisk in the remainder. The meringue must be glossy and form peaks when spoonfuls are dropped into the bowl. Fold in the black coffee.

Line a baking sheet with a large sheet of baking paper and spread the meringue mixture over the paper to form a 20 cm (8 inch) diameter round. Make a slight hollow in the centre of the meringue and cook in a preheated oven, 120°C (250°F), Gas Mark ½, for 1 hour until the meringue is crisp. Remove from the oven and leave to cool for about 10 minutes before peeling off the paper.

When the meringue is cold, fill the hollow in the top with the fromage frais. Arrange the cherries and nectarines chunks on top and serve immediately.

For berry & rosewater pavlova, make the meringue mixture as above, folding in ¼ teaspoon rosewater before placing it on the baking sheet and baking as above. Combine 250 g (8 oz) mixed fresh berries (such as strawberries, raspberries and blueberries) and stir in the rind and juice of ½ lemon. Use instead of the cherries and nectarines as a topping over the fromage frais.

apple & berry strudels

Calories per serving **102**
Serves **4**
Preparation time **15 minutes**
Cooking time **20 minutes**

2 **cooking apples**, peeled
    and grated
175 g (6 oz) **mixed berries**,
    plus extra to decorate
pinch of **ground cinnamon**
1 tablespoon **clear honey**
2 sheets of **filo pastry**
1 **egg white**, lightly beaten
mint sprigs, to decorate

Put the grated apples, berries, cinnamon and 1 teaspoon of the honey in a saucepan and cook gently for about 5 minutes or until the fruit is soft.

Brush the filo pastry sheets with the egg white and place 1 sheet on top of the other. Cut the sheets into quarters and place one-quarter of the fruit in the centre of each rectangle. Tuck in the ends of the pastry and roll into sausage shapes.

Place the strudels on a baking sheet, brush with the remaining honey and bake in a preheated oven, 150°C (300°F), Gas Mark 2, for 15 minutes or until golden.

Decorate the strudels with mint sprigs and extra berries and serve with a little low-fat custard, if liked (remembering to count the extra calories).

For summer apple & berry tartlets, cook the fruit as above. Cut each filo pastry sheet into 8 squares. Melt 20 g (¾ oz) unsalted butter in a saucepan. Brush each filo square with melted butter, then lay one square on top of a second, at a slight angle to the first. Place each double layer of filo in a hole of a bun tin to make 8 tartlet cases. Spoon the cooked fruit into the pastry cases and bake as above for 12–15 minutes until the pastry edges are golden. Decorate and serve as above.

tipsy blueberry & mascarpone pots

Calories per serving **146**
Serves **4**
Preparation time **15 minutes**,
   plus soaking and chilling

200 g (7 oz) blueberries
2 tablespoons **kirsch** or **vodka**
150 g (5 oz) **reduced-fat**
   mascarpone cheese
150 ml (5 fl oz) **low-fat**
   natural yogurt
2 tablespoons **granulated**
   sweetener
grated rind and juice of 1 **lime**

Combine 150 g (5 oz) of the blueberries with the alcohol in a bowl and leave to soak for at least 1 hour. Then mash the blueberries.

Beat together the mascarpone and yogurt in a separate bowl until smooth, then mix in the sweetener and the lime rind and juice.

Layer alternate spoonfuls of mashed blueberries and mascarpone in 4 glasses. Top with the whole blueberries and chill until ready to serve.

For mango pots with ricotta, replace the blueberries with 200 g (7 oz) cubed fresh mango and soak in 2 tablespoons vodka. To make the cream, replace the mascarpone with 200 g (7 oz) ricotta cheese and fold into the yogurt with 2 tablespoons clear honey instead of the granular sweetener. Add the lime rind and juice, then assemble the pots as above.

mango & passion fruit brûlées

Calories per serving **131**
Serves **2**
Preparation time **10 minutes**,
    plus cooling and chilling
Cooking time **1–2 minutes**

½ **small mango**, stoned,
    peeled and thinly sliced
1 **passion fruit**, halved and
    flesh scooped out
150 ml (¼ pint) **low-fat
    natural yogurt**
100 g (3½ oz) **low-fat (less
    than 3%) crème fraîche**
½ tablespoon **icing sugar**
a few drops of **vanilla extract**
1 tablespoon **demerara sugar**

Divide the mango between 2 ramekins. Mix together the passion fruit flesh, yogurt, crème fraîche, icing sugar and vanilla extract in a bowl, then spoon the mixture over the mango. Tap each ramekin to level the surface.

Sprinkle over the demerara sugar, then place the brûlées under a preheated hot grill and cook for 1–2 minutes until the sugar has melted. Leave to cool, then chill for about 30 minutes before serving.

For mango & passion fruit fools, purée the flesh of 1 mango in a blender or food processor and transfer to a bowl. Alternatively, rub the mango through a sieve to purée. Sieve the pulp from 2 passion fruits to remove the pips. Stir the passion fruit pulp into the mango purée, then stir in 200 ml (7 fl oz) 0% fat Greek yogurt. Spoon into 2 glasses and serve with lime wedges.

cakes & bakes

lemon & raspberry cupcakes

Calories per cupcake **206**
Makes **12**
Preparation time **10 minutes**
Cooking time **12–15 minutes**

150 g (5 oz) **butter**, softened
150 g (5 oz) **granulated sugar**
75 g (3 oz) **rice flour**
75 g (3 oz) **maize/cornflour**
1 tablespoon **baking powder**
grated rind and juice of
  1 lemon
3 **eggs**, beaten
125 g (4 oz) **raspberries**
1 tablespoon **lemon curd**

Line a large 12-hole muffin tin with large muffin cases. Place all the ingredients except the raspberries and lemon curd in a large bowl and whisk together using an electric hand whisk, or beat with a wooden spoon. Fold in the raspberries.

Spoon half of the mixture into the paper cases, dot over a little lemon curd, then add the remaining sponge mixture.

Bake in a preheated oven, 200°C (400°F), Gas Mark 6, for 12–15 minutes until golden and firm to the touch. Transfer to a wire rack to cool.

For chocolate & banana cupcakes, make the cupcake batter as above, replacing the raspberries with the chopped flesh of 1 ripe banana. Spoon half the mixture into the paper cases, then top with a small dollop of chocolate spread instead of the lemon curd. You will need about 1 tablespoon of spread in total. Top with the remaining batter and cook as above.

blackcurrant & almond muffins

Calories per muffin **153**
Makes **12**
Preparation time **5 minutes**
Cooking time **20–25 minutes**

200 g (7 oz) **plain flour**
2 teaspoons **baking powder**
½ teaspoon **bicarbonate
  of soda**
pinch of **salt**
50 g (2 oz) **caster sugar**
a few drops of **almond extract**
75 g (3 oz) **unsalted butter**,
  melted
200 ml (7 fl oz) **buttermilk**
300 g (10 oz) can
  **blackcurrants in natural
  juice**, drained, or 250 g
  (8 oz) fresh or frozen
  blackcurrants, thawed
40 g (1½ oz) **flaked almonds**

Line a 12-hole muffin tin with paper muffin cases.
Sift the flour, baking powder, bicarbonate of soda and
salt into a bowl, then stir in the sugar.

Mix together the almond extract, melted butter,
buttermilk and blackcurrants in a separate large bowl,
then very lightly stir in the dry ingredients. The mixture
should still look a little lumpy.

Spoon the mixture into the paper cases, sprinkle over
the flaked almonds, then bake in a preheated oven,
190°C (375°F), Gas Mark 5, for 20–25 minutes until
risen and golden. Transfer to a wire rack to cool.

For raspberry & coconut muffins, make the
muffin batter as above, omitting the almond extract
and replacing the blackcurrants with 250 g (8 oz)
fresh raspberries. Spoon into the muffin tin, omit the
flaked almonds and bake as above. Meanwhile, combine
2 tablespoons desiccated coconut and 1 teaspoon
caster sugar in a bowl with 1 tablespoon boiling water.
Spoon the coconut mixture over the muffins when they
come out of the oven, then cool on a wire rack.

chocolate mini muffins

Calories per muffin **71**
Makes **40**
Preparation time **30 minutes**,
  plus cooling
Cooking time **15 minutes**

200 g (7 oz) **brown rice flour**
2 tablespoons **chickpea/
  gram flour**
1 teaspoon **bicarbonate
  of soda**
2 teaspoons **baking powder**
½ teaspoon **xanthan gum**
125 g (4 oz) **golden caster
  sugar**
75 g (3 oz) **butter**, melted
1 **egg**, beaten
200 ml (7 fl oz) **buttermilk**
75 g (3 oz) **milk chocolate
  drops** or **milk chocolate**,
  chopped
75 g (3 oz) **milk chocolate**,
  to decorate

Line four 12-hole mini-muffin tins with 40 paper cases. Sift the flours, bicarbonate of soda, baking powder and xanthan gum into a large bowl, then stir in the sugar.

Mix together the melted butter, egg and buttermilk in a separate bowl. Gently combine the dry and wet ingredients, then lightly fold the milk chocolate drops or chopped milk chocolate into the mixture, stirring well.

Spoon the mixture into the paper cases and bake in a preheated oven, 200°C (400°F), Gas Mark 6, for 15 minutes until golden and risen. Transfer to a wire rack to cool.

Put the remaining milk chocolate in a heatproof bowl and melt over a saucepan of gently simmering water. Drizzle over the cooled muffins before serving.

For chocolate & orange mini muffins, make the muffin batter as above, replacing the milk chocolate drops with 2 tablespoons cocoa powder. Roughly chop 50 g (2 oz) candied orange peel and fold into the mixture before baking as above.

banoffee bites

Calories per bite **122**
Makes **24**
Preparation time **10 minutes**,
   plus cooling
Cooking time **10–12 minutes**

200 g (7 oz) **brown rice flour**
75 g (3 oz) **butter**, softened
75 g (3 oz) **golden caster
   sugar**
2 teaspoons **baking powder**
1 large **banana**, mashed
2 **eggs**
6 **toffees**, chopped

Topping

1 tablespoon **light
   muscovado sugar**
15 g (½ oz) **chewy banana
   slices** or **dried banana
   chips**

Line two 12-hole mini muffin tins with paper cases.
Place all the cake ingredients except the toffees in a
food processor and whiz until smooth, or beat in a large
bowl. Stir in the toffees.

Spoon the mixture into the paper cases, sprinkle over
most of the muscovado sugar and bake in a preheated
oven, 200°C (400°F), Gas Mark 6, for 10–12 minutes
until golden and just firm to the touch. Transfer to a wire
rack to cool.

Top the cooled cakes with chewy banana slices or
banana chips and sprinkle with the remaining sugar.

For butterfly banana & walnut mini muffins, make
the muffin mixture as above, replacing the toffees with
50 g (2 oz) roughly chopped walnuts. Bake as above,
then push 2 banana chip halves into each muffin, to
look like butterfly wings. Serve with a light dusting of
icing sugar instead of the muscovado sugar.

scrumptious strawberry scones

Calories per scone **292**
Makes **8**
Preparation time **10 minutes**,
  plus cooling
Cooking time **12 minutes**

175 g (6 oz) **rice flour**
75 g (3 oz) **potato flour**
1 teaspoon **xanthan gum**
1 teaspoon **baking powder**
1 teaspoon **bicarbonate
  of soda**
75 g (3 oz) **butter**, cubed
40 g (1½ oz) **caster sugar**
1 large **egg**, beaten
3 tablespoons **buttermilk**, plus
  a little extra for brushing
150 ml (¼ pint) **whipping
  cream**
250 g (8 oz) **strawberries**,
  lightly crushed

Place the flours, xanthan gum, baking powder,
bicarbonate of soda and butter in a food processor
and whiz until the mixture resembles fine breadcrumbs,
or rub in by hand in a large bowl.

Stir in the sugar. Using the blade of a knife, stir in the
egg and buttermilk until the mixture comes together.

Tip the dough out on to a lightly floured surface and
gently press it down to a thickness of 2.5 cm (1 inch).
Using a 5 cm (2 inch) cutter, cut out 8 scones.

Place on a lightly floured baking sheet, brush with a
little buttermilk, then bake in a preheated oven, 220°C
(425°F), Gas Mark 7, for about 12 minutes until golden
and risen. Transfer to a wire rack to cool.

Meanwhile, whisk the cream until it forms fairly firm
peaks and fold in the strawberries. Slice the scones in
half and fill with the strawberry cream.

For raisin scones with blackcurrant cream, make
the scones as above, adding 50 g (2 oz) raisins to the
raw mixture before shaping. Bake and cool as above.
Omit the cream and strawberries. Fold 3 tablespoons
blackcurrant compote into 150 ml (¼ pint) fat-free
natural fromage frais and use to fill the scones.

fruity mango flapjacks

Calories per flapjack **219**
Makes **12**
Preparation time **10 minutes**
Cooking time **35 minutes**

100 g (3½ oz) **soft light brown sugar**
150 g (5 oz) **butter**
2 tablespoons **golden syrup**
200 g (7 oz) **millet flakes**
2 tablespoons **mixed seeds**, such as pumpkin and sunflower
75 g (3 oz) **dried mango**, roughly chopped

Place the sugar, butter and syrup in a heavy-based saucepan and heat until melted, then stir in the remaining ingredients.

Spoon the mixture into a 28 x 18 cm (11 x 7 inch) nonstick baking tin, press down lightly and bake in a preheated oven, 150°C (300°F), Gas Mark 2, for 30 minutes.

Mark into 12 pieces, then cool before removing from the tin. Cut or break into 12 pieces once cooled.

For honey & ginger flapjacks, place 50 g (2 oz) soft light brown sugar in a pan with 50 g (2 oz) clear honey and the butter. Omit the golden syrup. Heat until melted, then add the millet flakes or 200 g (7 oz) porridge oats and the seeds. Instead of the dried mango, stir in 1 ball of stem ginger, finely chopped. Spoon the mixture into the tin and continue as above.

apricot, fig & mixed seed bites

Calories per bite **107**
Makes **24**
Preparation time **10 minutes**
Cooking time **10–15 minutes**

150 g (5 oz) **polyunsaturated margarine**
75 g (3 oz) **soft light brown sugar**
1 **egg**, beaten
2 tablespoons **water**
75 g (3 oz) **plain wholemeal flour**
½ teaspoon **bicarbonate of soda**
100 g (3½ oz) **rolled oats**
50 g (2 oz) **ready-to-eat dried apricots**, chopped
50 g (2 oz) **dried figs**, chopped
50 g (2 oz) **mixed seeds**, such as pumpkin, sunflower and sesame

Line 2 baking sheets with nonstick baking paper.

Beat together the margarine and sugar in a bowl until light and fluffy, then beat in the egg and measurement water.

Sift the flour and bicarbonate of soda into the bowl, adding any bran in the sieve. Add the oats, apricots, figs and seeds, then fold all the ingredients into the margarine and sugar mixture.

Place 24 walnut-sized pieces of the mixture on the baking sheets and flatten them slightly with the back of a fork.

Bake the bites in a preheated oven, 180°C (350°F), Gas Mark 4, for 10–15 minutes until golden. Transfer to a wire rack to cool.

For citrus fig & pine nut bites, beat together the margarine and sugar, then beat in the egg and 2 tablespoons orange juice instead of the water. Combine the remaining ingredients in a bowl, as above, replacing the apricots with 50 g (2 oz) chopped citrus peel, and the mixed seeds with 50 g (2 oz) pine nuts. Shape and cook as above.

mini orange shortbreads

Calories per shortbread **30**
Makes **80**
Preparation time **10 minutes**,
  plus cooling
Cooking time **10–12 minutes**

250 g (8 oz) **plain flour**, sifted
175 g (6 oz) **unsalted butter**,
  cut into small pieces
grated rind of **1 orange**
½ teaspoon **mixed spice**
75 g (3 oz) **caster sugar**
2 teaspoons **cold water**

To serve
2 teaspoons **icing sugar**
1 teaspoon **cocoa powder**

Place the flour in a bowl, add the butter and rub in with the fingertips until the mixture resembles fine breadcrumbs. Stir in the remaining ingredients with the measurement water and mix to form a dough.

Roll out the dough on a lightly floured surface to a thickness of 2.5 mm (⅛ inch). Using a 1.5 cm (¾ inch) plain cutter, cut out about 80 rounds.

Place the rounds on nonstick baking sheets and bake in a preheated oven, 200°C (400°F), Gas Mark 6, for 10–12 minutes until golden. Carefully transfer to a wire rack to cool.

Mix together the icing sugar and cocoa powder and dust a little over the shortbreads before serving.

For cardamom & rosewater mini shortbreads, crush 5 cardamom pods and pick out the seeds. Discard the pods. Grind the seeds in a pestle and mortar and place in a bowl with the flour and butter. Rub together the flour and butter as above, then add the orange, sugar, 1 ½ teaspoons cold water and ½ teaspoon rosewater, omitting the mixed spice. Bring the dough together, then roll out and bake as above. Serve dusted with icing sugar, omitting the cocoa powder.

cranberry & hazelnut cookies

Calories per cookie **60**
Makes **30**
Preparation time **10 minutes**
Cooking time **5–6 minutes**

50 g (2 oz) **unsalted butter,**
softened, or **polyunsaturated**
margarine
40 g (1½ oz) **granulated**
sugar
25 g (1 oz) **soft light**
brown sugar
1 **egg,** beaten
a few drops of **vanilla extract**
150 g (5 oz) **self-raising**
flour, sifted
50 g (2 oz) **rolled oats**
50 g (2 oz) **dried cranberries**
40 g (1½ oz) **hazelnuts,**
toasted and chopped

Line 2 baking sheets with nonstick baking paper.

Beat together the butter, sugars, egg and vanilla extract in a large bowl until smooth.

Stir in the flour and oats, then the dried cranberries and chopped hazelnuts.

Place 30 teaspoonfuls of the mixture on to the baking sheets and flatten them slightly with the back of a fork.

Bake in a preheated oven, 180°C (350°F), Gas Mark 4, for about 5–6 minutes until browned. Transfer to a wire rack to cool.

For dark chocolate & ginger cookies, prepare the mixture as above, omitting the cranberries and hazelnuts. Replace them with 40 g (1½ oz) dark chocolate drops and 2 pieces of chopped stem ginger or ½ teaspoon of peeled and grated fresh root ginger. Stir together and bake as above.

white chocolate drops

Calories per biscuit **98**

Makes **20**

Preparation time **10 minutes**,
   plus chilling and cooling

Cooking time **20 minutes**

50 g (2 oz) **white vegetable fat**

50 g (2 oz) **butter**, softened

50 g (2 oz) **caster sugar**

1 **egg yolk**

200 g (7 oz) **brown rice flour**

1 tablespoon **ground almonds**

50 g (2 oz) **white chocolate**,
   grated

2 teaspoons **icing sugar**,
   to serve

Place the fats and sugar in a large bowl and beat together, then beat in the egg yolk followed by the remaining ingredients. Form the dough into a ball, wrap closely in clingfilm and chill for 1 hour.

Remove the dough from the refrigerator, unwrap and place on a lightly floured surface. Knead the dough a little to soften it, then divide into 20 balls.

Place the balls on 2 baking sheets, flatten them slightly with a fork and bake in a preheated oven, 180°C (350°F), Gas Mark 4, for about 20 minutes until golden. Transfer to a wire rack to cool. Dust over a little icing sugar before serving.

For chocolate & coconut bites, make the biscuits as above, omitting the ground almonds. Place 50 g (2 oz) plain chocolate in a heatproof bowl and melt over a saucepan of gently simmering water. Dip one-quarter of each cooled biscuit in the chocolate, then dip the chocolate-coated edge of the biscuits in 50 g (2 oz) desiccated coconut. Place on a tray in the refrigerator for 20 minutes to allow the chocolate to set, then store the biscuits in an airtight container. There will be plenty of leftover chocolate and coconut, but you will need this quantity so that the job of dipping the biscuits is not too fiddly.

orange & polenta crispy cookies

Calories per cookie **67**
Makes **20**
Preparation time **10 minutes**,
  plus chilling
Cooking time **8 minutes**

75 g (3 oz) **polenta**
25 g (1 oz) **rice flour**
25 g (1 oz) **ground almonds**
½ teaspoon **baking powder**
75 g (3 oz) **icing sugar**
50 g (2 oz) **butter**, cubed
1 **egg yolk**, beaten
grated rind 1 **orange**
25 g (1 oz) **flaked almonds**

Line 2 baking sheets with nonstick baking paper. Place the polenta, flour, ground almonds, baking powder, icing sugar and butter in a food processor and whiz until the mixture resembles fine breadcrumbs, or rub in by hand in a large bowl.

Stir in the egg yolk and orange rind and bring together to make a dough. Wrap closely in clingfilm and chill for 30 minutes.

Remove the dough from the refrigerator, unwrap and roll out thinly on a lightly floured surface. Cut into 20 rounds with a 4 cm (1½ inch) cutter. Transfer to the prepared baking sheets, sprinkle with the flaked almonds and bake in a preheated oven, 180°C (350°F), Gas Mark 4, for about 8 minutes until golden. Leave the cookies to cool on the sheets for a few minutes to harden, then transfer to a wire rack to cool.

For Christmasy polenta cookies, prepare the dough as above, adding ¼ teaspoon vanilla extract and ½ teaspoon each of ground cinnamon and mixed spice when stirring in the egg. Chill and roll out as above, then use a star-shaped cookie cutter to cut out the cookies. Place on baking sheets lined with nonstick baking paper and cook as above, omitting the flaked almonds.

lemon, pistachio & date squares

Calories per square **174**
Makes **20**
Preparation time **10 minutes**,
    plus cooling and chilling
Cooking time **20 minutes**

grated rind of 1 **lemon**
75 g (3 oz) **ready-to-eat
    dried dates**, chopped
75 g (3 oz) **unsalted
    pistachio nuts**, chopped
75 g (3 oz) **flaked almonds**,
    chopped
125 g (4 oz) **soft light
    brown sugar**
150 g (5 oz) **millet flakes**
40 g (1½ oz) **cornflakes**,
    lightly crushed
400 g (13 oz) can **low-fat
    condensed milk**
25 g (1 oz) **mixed seeds**,
    such as pumpkin
    and sunflower

Simply place all the ingredients in a large bowl and mix together. Spoon into a 28 x 18 cm (11 x 7 inch) baking tin and spread evenly. Bake in a preheated oven, 180°C (350°F), Gas Mark 4, for 20 minutes.

Leave to cool in the tin, then mark into 20 squares and chill until firm.

For chocolate & almond squares, make the mixture as above, omitting the pistachios and flaked almonds. Roughly chop 100 g (3½ oz) blanched almonds and add to the mixture with 65 g (2½ oz) bran flakes and 50 g (2 oz) melted plain chocolate. Cook and cool, mark and chill as above, drizzling the top with melted white chocolate once cooled, if liked.

passion cake squares

Calories per square **307**
Makes **16**
Preparation time **10 minutes**,
  plus cooling
Cooking time **1 hour**

175 g (6 oz) **brown rice flour**
375 g (12 oz) **caster sugar**
2 teaspoons **baking powder**
1 teaspoon **xanthan gum**
1 teaspoon **ground cinnamon**
150 ml (¼ pint) **rapeseed** or
  corn oil
2 **eggs**, beaten
a few drops of **vanilla extract**
375 g (12 oz) **carrots**, grated
50 g (2 oz) **desiccated
  coconut**
100 g (3½ oz) **canned
  crushed pineapple**, drained
50 g (2 oz) **sultanas**

Topping
200 g (7 oz) **low-fat cream
  cheese**
2 tablespoons **clear honey**
75 g (3 oz) **walnuts**, chopped
  (optional)

Grease and flour a 20 cm (8 inch) square cake tin.
Sift the flour, sugar, baking powder, xanthan gum and
cinnamon into a large bowl. Add the oil, eggs and vanilla
extract and beat well.

Fold in the carrots, coconut, pineapple and sultanas
and spoon the mixture into the prepared tin. Bake in a
preheated oven, 180°C (350°F), Gas Mark 4, for about
1 hour or until a skewer inserted in the middle comes
out clean. Leave to cool in the tin.

Beat together the cream cheese and honey and smooth
over the cake, then sprinkle the nuts, if using, on top.
Cut into 16 squares.

For tropical cake squares, prepare the cake batter as
in the first step above, omitting the cinnamon. Peel and
stone 1 small ripe mango and roughly chop it. Fold it
into the batter with the carrots, coconut and 50 g (2 oz)
chopped Brazil nuts. Omit the pineapple and sultanas.
Bake and cool as above. For the topping, fold the flesh
of 3 passion fruits into the cream cheese, sweeten
with honey to taste, then spread over the cake. Cut into
squares, omitting the walnuts.

moist banana & carrot cake

Calories per serving **183**
Serves **14**
Preparation time **10 minutes**,
   plus cooling
Cooking time **1 hour**
   40 minutes

175 g (6 oz) **ready-to-eat
   dried apricots**, roughly
   chopped
125 ml (4 fl oz) **water**
1 **egg**
2 tablespoons **clear honey**
100 g (3½ oz) **walnuts**,
   roughly chopped
500 g (1 lb) ripe **bananas**,
   mashed
1 large **carrot**, about 125 g
   (4 oz), grated
225 g (7½ oz) **self-raising
   flour**, sifted

Topping
150 g (5 oz) **low-fat cream
   cheese**
2 tablespoons **lemon curd**

Grease and line a 1 kg (2 lb) loaf tin. Place the apricots in a small saucepan with the measurement water, bring to the boil, then reduce the heat and simmer for 10 minutes. Transfer to a blender or food processor and blend to form a thick purée.

Put all the remaining cake ingredients in a large bowl and add the apricot purée. Mix well, then spoon into the tin.

Bake in a preheated oven, 180°C (350°F), Gas Mark 4, for 1½ hours or until a skewer inserted in the middle comes out clean. Turn out on to a wire rack to cool.

Beat together the cream cheese and lemon curd in a bowl, then spread over the top of the cooled loaf. Serve cut into 14 slices.

For date & banana cake, replace the apricots with 150 g (5 oz) dates. Cook and purée as above, reducing the water to 75 ml (3 fl oz). Make the cake batter with all the above ingredients, using the date purée instead of the apricot and adding 2 teaspoons mixed spice. Bake and leave to cool as above. Combine 1 teaspoon ground cinnamon with 2 tablespoons golden caster sugar and dust over the cake, instead of the lemon topping.

chocolate, courgette & nut cake

Calories per serving **237**
Serves **12**
Preparation time **10 minutes**,
   plus cooling
Cooking time **40 minutes**

250 g (8 oz) **courgettes**,
   coarsely grated
2 **eggs**
100 ml (3½ fl oz) **vegetable oil**
grated rind and juice of
   1 orange
125 g (4 oz) **caster sugar**
225 g (7½ oz) **self-raising
   flour**
2 tablespoons **cocoa powder**
½ teaspoon **bicarbonate
   of soda**
½ teaspoon **baking powder**
50 g (2 oz) **ready-to-eat dried
   apricots**, chopped

Topping
200 g (7 oz) **low-fat cream
   cheese**
2 tablespoons **chocolate
   hazelnut spread**
1 tablespoon **hazelnuts**,
   toasted and chopped

Grease and line a 20 cm (8 inch) deep loose-bottomed cake tin. Place the courgettes in a sieve and squeeze out any excess liquid.

Beat together the eggs, vegetable oil, orange rind and juice and sugar in a large bowl. Sift in the flour, cocoa powder, bicarbonate of soda and baking powder and beat to combine.

Fold in the courgettes and apricots, then spoon the mixture into the prepared tin.

Bake in a preheated oven, 180°C (350°F), Gas Mark 4, for 40 minutes until risen and firm to the touch. Turn out on to a wire rack to cool.

Beat together the cream cheese and chocolate hazelnut spread in a bowl, then spread over the top of the cake. Sprinkle over the hazelnuts and serve cut into 12 slices.

For strawberry & fromage frais topping, to use instead of the chocolate and hazelnut topping, blend 100 g (3½ oz) strawberries in a blender or food processor with 1 tablespoon clear honey to make a purée. Stir in 125 g (4 oz) fat-free natural fromage frais and spread over the top of the cooled cake. Decorate the top of the cake with halved strawberries, if liked.

olive & haloumi bread

Calories per serving **189**
Serves **12**
Preparation time **15 minutes**,
   plus proving
Cooking time **35 minutes**

500 g (1 lb) **strong plain
   flour**, plus extra for sifting
7 g (¼ oz) sachet **fast-action
   dried yeast**
pinch of **salt**
2 tablespoons **olive oil**
300 ml (½ pint) **warm water**
1 **onion**, thinly sliced
100 g (3½ oz) **pitted olives**
75 g (3 oz) **low-fat haloumi
   cheese**, chopped
2 tablespoons chopped
   parsley

Place the flour, yeast and salt in a large bowl. Combine half the oil with the measurement water in a jug and stir into the flour to form a dough.

Turn the dough out on a lightly floured surface and knead for 5 minutes until smooth and elastic. Place in a lightly oiled bowl, cover with a damp cloth and set aside in a warm place for about 1 hour until doubled in size.

Meanwhile, heat the remaining oil in a frying pan, add the onion and fry for 7–8 minutes until softened and golden. Leave to cool.

Turn the risen dough out on the floured surface and add the remaining ingredients, including the onion, kneading it into the dough. Shape into an oval, place on a lightly floured baking sheet and leave to rise for 1 hour.

When the loaf has risen, slash a few cuts in the top, sift over a little flour, then bake in a preheated oven, 220°C (425°F), Gas Mark 7, for about 25 minutes until hollow-sounding when tapped. Transfer to a wire rack to cool.

For olive & sun-blush tomato swirls, make the dough and leave to rise until doubled in size. Fry the onions in the oil as above, then stir in the olives, 75 g (3 oz) sun-blush tomatoes and ½ teaspoon fennel seeds and leave to cool. Roll the dough out on a floured surface to the size of an A4 sheet of paper and spread with the olive, onion and tomato mix. Roll up the dough from one long end and cut the roll into 12 rounds. Lay them on a large baking sheet dusted with flour, cover with a damp cloth and leave to rise for 30 minutes. Bake in a preheated oven, 220°C (425°F), Gas Mark 7, for 12–15 minutes until golden.

feta & herb loaf

Calories per serving **118**
Serves **14**
Preparation time **10 minutes**,
    plus proving
Cooking time **45 minutes**

200 g (7 oz) **polenta**
100 g (3½ oz) **rice flour**
50 g (2 oz) **dried milk powder**
pinch of **salt**
7 g (¼ oz) sachet **fast-action
    dried yeast**
2 teaspoons **caster sugar**
2 teaspoons **xanthan gum**
3 **eggs**, beaten
2 tablespoons chopped
    mixed herbs
450 ml (¾ pint) **tepid water**
100 g (3½ oz) **feta cheese**,
    crumbled

Grease and line a 1 kg (2 lb) loaf tin. Sift the polenta, flour, milk powder and salt into a large bowl and stir well to combine. Stir in the yeast, sugar and xanthan gum.

Place the eggs, herbs and measurement water in a bowl and mix together. Stir this mixture into the dry ingredients and combine to form a soft dough. Beat for 5 minutes, then stir in the feta cheese.

Spoon the mixture into the prepared tin, cover with a clean damp tea towel and leave in a warm place to rise for about 30 minutes until the mixture is near the top of the tin. Bake in a preheated oven, 180°C (350°F), Gas Mark 4, for about 45 minutes until brown and hollow-sounding when tapped. Transfer to a wire rack to cool.

For polenta, spinach & chilli loaf, make the dough as above, replacing the feta cheese with 100 g (3½ oz) cooked spinach (squeezed dry in a tea towel, then finely chopped), 1 teaspoon caraway seeds and 1 deseeded and finely chopped red chilli. Leave to rise in the tin, bake and cool as above.

nutty seed loaf

Calories per serving **263**
Serves **8**
Preparation time **10 minutes**
Cooking time **25 minutes**

400 g (13 oz) **brown rice flour**,
  plus extra for sifting
25 g (1 oz) **rice bran**
2 tablespoons **dried milk
  powder**
½ teaspoon **bicarbonate
  of soda**
1 teaspoon **baking powder**
½–1 teaspoon **salt**
1 teaspoon **xanthan gum**
pinch of **caster sugar**
50 g (2 oz) **mixed seeds**,
  such as sunflower and
  pumpkin
50 g (2 oz) **hazelnuts**, toasted
  and roughly chopped
1 **egg**, lightly beaten
300 ml (½ pint) **buttermilk**

Place all the dry ingredients in a large bowl and mix together. In a separate bowl, mix together the egg and buttermilk, then stir into the dry ingredients.

Tip the dough out on to a lightly floured surface and form into a round about 20 cm (8 inches) in diameter. Mark into 8 segments, then place on a baking sheet and sift over a little extra flour.

Place in an oven preheated to its highest setting and cook for 10 minutes, then reduce the heat to 200°C (400°F), Gas Mark 6, and continue to cook for about 15 minutes until golden and sounding hollow when tapped. Transfer to a wire rack to cool.

For seeded Parmesan buns, make the dough as above, using 50 g (2 oz) sesame seeds instead of the mixed seeds, and replacing the hazelnuts with 50 g (2 oz) grated Parmesan cheese. Shape the dough into 8 round buns, then place on a baking sheet and dust with a little extra flour. Bake for 10 minutes as above, then reduce the oven heat as above and cook for a further 8–10 minutes until the buns sound hollow when tapped.

index

acknowledgements

Recipe Consultant: Angela Dowden
Commissioning Editor: Eleanor Maxfield
Senior Editor: Leanne Bryan
Designer: Eoghan O'Brien
Design: Jeremy Tilston
Picture Library Manager: Jen Veall
Production Controller: Sarah Kramer

Picture Acknowledgements
Octopus Publishing Group Stephen Conroy 10, 59, 61,
67, 89, 145, 147, 161, 163; Will Heap 164-165; David
Munns 46-47; Emma Neish 175, 201, 207, 209, 211,
221, 223, 225, 233, 235; Lis Parsons 1, 15, 16, 17,
21, 25, 81, 87, 93, 107, 109, 113, 125, 131, 137, 141,
143, 155, 157, 159, 167, 171, 179, 181, 185, 197, 203,
213, 217, 227, 229, 231; William Reavell 4-5, 33, 103,
115, 133; Craig Robertson 29, 37, 39, 51, 97; Gareth
Sambidge 63, 193; William Shaw 2-3, 6-7, 12, 23, 27,
31, 35, 41, 43, 45, 49, 53, 55, 57, 65, 69, 71, 73, 75, 77,
79, 83, 85, 91, 95, 111, 117, 121, 123, 127, 135, 139,
149, 151, 153, 169, 173, 177, 183, 187, 189, 191, 195,
205, 215, 219; Eleanor Skan 13; Simon Smith 99, 101,
119, 129; Ian Wallace 18-19, 104-105, 198-199.